CW01618778

The Bea
FISHING

Alan Wrangles

Illustrated by John Reynolds

Beaver Books

First published in 1981 by
The Hamlyn Publishing Group Limited
London · New York · Sydney · Toronto
Astronaut House, Feltham, Middlesex, England
(Paperback Division: Hamlyn Paperbacks, Banda House,
Cambridge Grove, Hammersmith, London W6 0LE)

© Copyright Text Alan Wrangles 1981
© Copyright Illustrations
The Hamlyn Publishing Group Limited 1981

ISBN 0 600 20207 0

Filmset, printed and bound in Great Britain by
Hazell Watson & Viney Limited, Aylesbury, Bucks
Set in Times Roman

To my grandson, James Marcus, in the hope that he too will enjoy fishing.

All rights reserved. This book is sold subject to the condition that it shall not in any manner be lent, re-sold, hired or otherwise circulated without the publisher's prior consent in writing in any form of binding or cover other than that in which it is published and without a similar condition including this condition being imposed on the subsequent purchaser. No part of the book may be reproduced, stored in a retrieval system, or transmitted, in any form or by any electronic, mechanical, photocopying or recording means, or otherwise, without the publisher's prior consent in writing.

Contents

Acknowledgements

I am most grateful to Richard Barder, Brian Robertshaw, Brian Watts and Ken Whitehead for their specialist contributions to this book.

A.W.

Introduction

Alan Wrangles

Hunters become successful by learning all they can about their quarry, and the animals they hunt are either taught to be wary by their parents, or are provided by nature with various senses which automatically warn of danger.

Fish are complex creatures equipped with 'early warning' systems based on inter-related senses of smell and taste, as well as sight and sound. Different kinds of fish have varying degrees of the different senses. Nature places emphasis on that which is of the greatest benefit to the particular species. For example, pike (fish which live by hunting and scavenging) have large eyes set high on a flattened snout, which can look forward and focus on a prey. Many other species are not so equipped, indeed some such as eels and tench have relatively small eyes, but as they find their food mainly by smell and taste, sharp eyesight is not so essential. Therefore tench, eels and many other kinds of fish have highly developed tasting organs which assist their search for the food they eat.

All these facts are of the greatest importance to the angler, in both sea and freshwater. They not only help when choosing an area in which to fish, but also explain why certain baits, or even methods of fishing, are most likely to be successful.

Fish have inborn instincts to react to warnings of danger which can come from all sides. For example, birds like herons and gulls attack from above, while other fish and also animals such as otters, mink and seals can prey on them under water.

Only a very small percentage of fish which survive even as far as the 'fry' stage actually live to maturity. This being so, nature has compensated for this enormous and ever-continuing loss by providing fish with the facility of producing vast quantities of eggs. For example, a good size female ling weighing perhaps 9 kg (20 lb) or so, can produce as many as sixty million eggs.

Ling, a sea fish which feeds almost exclusively on other fish, becomes mature and will start laying eggs when it is about three years old, and approximately 50 cm (20 in) long.

Not all are as prolific as ling. Another well-known sea species, cod, do not produce anywere near as many eggs. A female weighing about 9 kg (20 lb) will shed some six million in her lifetime, and a 1-kg (2-lb) female flounder perhaps as many as two million.

Freshwater species such as chub and perch both lay similar quantities, perhaps 150,000 to 200,000 eggs; whereas roach will lay at best perhaps not many more than 14,000.

By the laying of such incredible numbers of eggs, nature does its best to make sure that the various kinds of fish survive, but this is not the only way in which it seeks to offer protection to animals exposed to predators.

Camouflage is an art we humans have learned from animals. Generally speaking, fish have a body colouring which enables them to blend with the type of background they normally inhabit.

Viewed from above, the speckled body of a trout becomes almost invisible against a river bed of stone and gravel, and frequently it is only the dark beady eyes of a flounder that betrays its presence as it lies in the mud. However, long before you have seen them, you will have been spotted by the fish.

Pike have wonderful camouflage: bodies with greenish-yellow spots and bars, with the darker wavy lines on the fins and a deeper greenish-brown back combining magnificently to make them almost invisible in their natural habitat among the reeds and underwater vegetation.

Both hunter and hunted need camouflage in order to survive. In the case of the pike, not only is its colouring a protection against its enemies (small pike are eaten by larger ones), but by merging into the background, the other fish and even water fowl on which it preys may not spot the lurking danger until it's too late.

Fish are also able to use soundwaves for both finding food and evading danger.

Unlike land animals they have a 'lateral line' – a kind of canal which runs along both flanks of the fish, covered with scales which have openings at set intervals. Vibrations created by, for example, footsteps on the bank, a waterfall, or the irregular flutterings of a sick fish struggling to hold its position in the stream, are transmitted through the water and picked up by the nerve ends in the 'canal'.

The vibrations pass through the openings or perforations in the scales covering the 'canal', and the fish's nervous system then interprets them.

Scientists are of the opinion that this particular system is far more finely tuned in predatory species like pike and perch than it is in a more sedentary kind such as carp. This is a fact which the angler can use to advantage. A spinner or plug fished in an erratic manner might well produce a sound like that which is transmitted by a sick or injured fish as it thrashes about awkwardly. A fish in this condition is soon taken by a predator and if the predator mistakes the spinner for its prey, it may easily be caught!

However useful the lateral line mechanism is to some hunters, it has not the same priority among those kinds of fish which root in the river bed and browse, sheep-like, on the weeds, or among those who feed principally at night.

For these, the ability to smell and/or taste is of the utmost importance, although vibrations from heavy footsteps still affect them. Talking, or other airborne sounds do not carry down to the fish. Eels, burbot, carp and tench are among those which rely heavily on the senses of smell and taste.

Barbels are another kind of sensory organ which help

fish to find suitable food. They are fleshy mouth appendages which distinguish edible food from other material as the fish root like pigs on the river bed.

Cod and mullet are two well-known kinds of sea fish which have barbels similar to those which are present on freshwater species such as carp, and indeed on the barbel itself, a highly prized sport fish of fairly limited distribution.

Taste buds are present not only on the barbels, but are found, according to the species, in various parts of the surface of the body, on the tongue, the lips, gill rakers, and so on. Therefore there is no need for a fish to actually take something into its mouth to discover whether or not it is an acceptable item of food.

A bait which is impregnated, or even just tainted, by a substance which is alien to the fish is far more likely to be ignored than one which is seemingly 'natural'. For example, bread paste made with water straight from the pond or river where you are fishing will be accepted by the fish more readily than paste made with water tasting of chlorine. Similarly, a clean maggot is usually more successful than a stale, evil-smelling one.

Unlike us, fish do not have passages connecting the nose and mouth; however, their nasal organ is very efficient, and in some cases is capable of detecting a smell from the most minute particle imaginable. Shark provide a good example of this fact; the stories regarding shark being attracted to blood are legion.

The fish's nasal opening leads to a chamber where substances of interest, which are carried in by the flow of water, are detected by the olfactory or 'smelling' cells. These cells are linked to the brain, and if the fish finds the smell attractive then it just 'follows its nose'.

Shark anglers make use of the fish's sense of smell by using a 'rubby-dubby' whilst fishing. This is, in essence, a wide-weave sack filled with evil-smelling minced fish offal with maybe some bran plus an amount of fish oil added for bulk and smell.

It's interesting to note that some shark-boat skippers

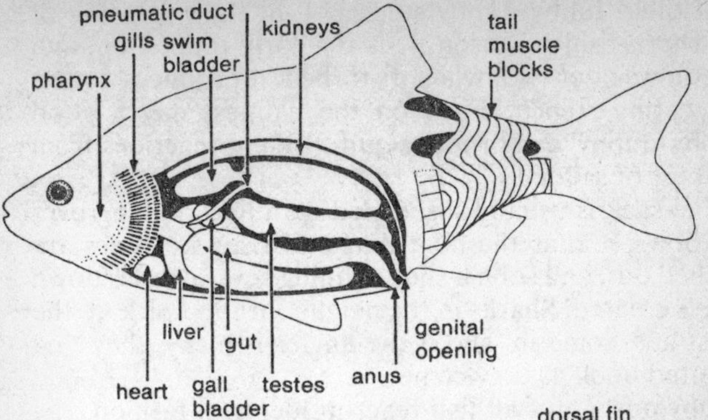
pneumatic duct
gills
swim bladder
kidneys
tail muscle blocks
pharynx
liver
gut
genital opening
anus
heart
gall bladder
testes

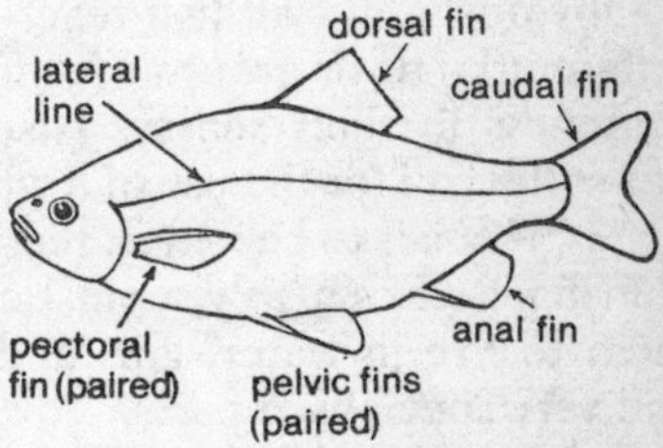
dorsal fin
lateral line
caudal fin
anal fin
pectoral fin (paired)
pelvic fins (paired)

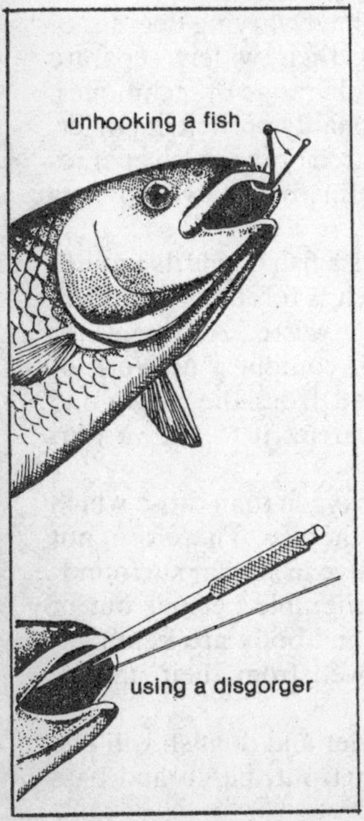
unhooking a fish
using a disgorger

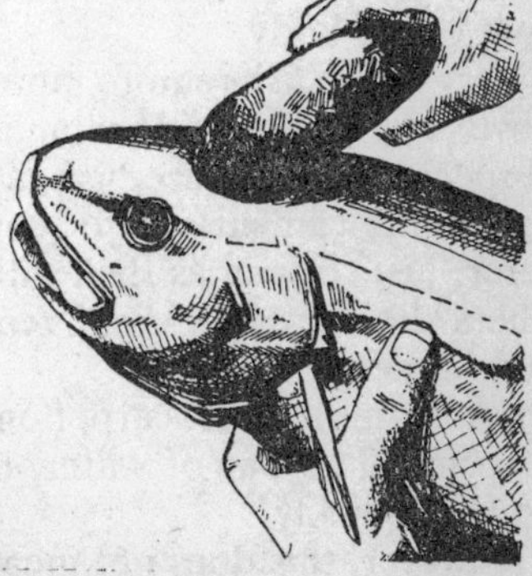
a fish is killed with a blow on the back of the head

start their ‘rubby-dubby stock pot’ at the beginning of the shark-fishing season. It is regularly topped up, and after a week or two, when disturbed, it produces a most nauseating stench. Even on the calmest day a good ‘rubby-dubby’ can produce quite violent reactions from the best of sailors!

The sack is usually suspended on a line running over the bows, and as the boat dips and rises so pieces are washed out, and soon a slick running several miles down tide is created. Sharks in the neighbourhood pick up the scent and home in, and if the angler is lucky, they find a baited hook as they come.

Obviously, not all fish react in identical fashion; the different kinds or groups of fish have varying degrees of acuteness in their senses. Also, their widely separate life-styles call for the use of a whole range of techniques, that is, if one is to become a reasonably proficient angler.

Fish possess a highly sophisticated body which enables them to live in water, gills and fins being two obvious and very specialised parts.

Fish breathe with their gills. As a fish opens its mouth, water is drawn in, and in closing it is forced over the gill filaments and then out again as waste. As the water passes over the filaments, which contain a network of blood vessels, oxygen is removed from the water and absorbed by the blood, which carries it to the various parts of the body.

Very active fish require more oxygen than those which move around slowly, feeding as they go. Therefore, not all species of freshwater fish can live in similar surroundings. Some can survive for considerable periods out of water, just so long as their gills and body are kept wet; others die very quickly if removed from their natural environment.

For example, eels, carp, flounder and dogfish will live for some time out of water, but trout, perch and bass die very quickly.

However, this does not mean that you can ignore the needs of fish, nor that you can opt out of the responsibility of killing, quickly and humanely, any fish you are keeping for food.

Basically, coarse fish, e.g. roach, dace, carp, bream, tench – all those freshwater species not belonging to the salmon and trout family – should be returned to the water as soon as possible after being caught. You should hold them carefully but firmly, with a wet cloth between your hand and the fish's body, and use a disgorger or a pair of long-nosed pliers to remove the hook. As fish are 'cold blooded' animals, you should not hold them with bare hands, or the heat from your hands will be akin to us sustaining a burn or scald.

If coarse fish need to be kept until they are weighed, for example, when competing in a match, put each one as it is caught into a keep-net of good size. Most, if not all, clubs lay down minimum sizes for such nets. Make sure the net is kept well down in the water.

A fish's lips, mouth and throat are not the highly sensitive areas that ours are. Indeed, some fish have lips so tough they can prize mussels from rocks.

Most fish bolt their food down whole, the crushing being done by teeth within their mouth or in the pharynx, a part of the throat. Carp, chub, dace and roach have teeth in the pharynx.

Some sea species have teeth at the entrance to the gullet as well as around the upper and lower jaws – they can also be set into the palate or roof of the mouth. Some teeth are shaped for grinding, others for cutting – it all depends how and what the species eats.

But once again this is information of value to the angler. For example, it is a wise fisherman who keeps his fingers out of a pike's mouth, and when fishing for ray or skate, a steel wire trace is necessary to prevent the fish from severing the line.

Knowing about a fish's mouth is important, not only because it can be dangerous to remove the hook, but also because it highlights the importance of using the right hook and of keeping it sharp.

If the fish is badly damaged as a result of being caught,

or if it is to be eaten, then it should be killed at once. *Never put a live fish into a plastic bag and leave it.*

You, having caught the fish, are totally responsible for it. If it is to be killed, hold it firmly and give it a sharp blow on the back of the head either with a priest or a similar object. As a general rule, a fish damaged whilst being caught or unhooked should be killed, otherwise disease will almost certainly attack, and the fish will die slowly.

The foregoing information will have given you some idea of how complicated and fascinating a fish's body is. If only one part fails to function correctly then it will die, possibly from disease, perhaps from starvation, or, most likely, it will be eaten by a predator.

Fish often have a protective coating of slime or mucus, which provides a defence against various harmful organisms. It is thus very important to handle fish correctly, for it is very easy to damage fins, scales and even various internal organs.

So, if you want to weigh your catch, or a single large fish, and return it to the water, unharmed, never place the hook on a spring-balance into the gill-opening or mouth. Always carry a square of fine mesh net, or put the fish into a large, but wet, plastic bag, and then weigh it. If you are concerned about the extra odd ounce or two, then weigh the net or bag separately and work out the accurate weight when the fish is back in the water. Fish handled properly suffer no harm, many have been caught on a number of occasions, but they still thrive.

Generally speaking, both game (trout and salmon) and sea fish are eaten, and so when they are caught, kill them quickly and put them into a bag – and keep the bag out of the sun and as cool as possible. A day in the summer's sun will reduce a prime fresh fish into a miserable stale mess.

And so to the question of cost, a most important factor, but one which is really very difficult to define.

The cheapest kind of fishing, sea fishing, is free, except for charges such as those made by the owners of a pier. Here one pays for the privilege of going on to it and using it as a place from which to fish. No licences or permits are needed for shore fishing, and it is generally accepted that all have the right to fish in tidal waters for sea fish. There are places where access or fishing rights are limited, naval dockyards for example, but this is really just a matter of common sense.

Bait digging is normally unrestricted, except where there are boat moorings or perhaps sea defence works which could be damaged if digging were allowed.

Sea anglers must pay heed to the law regarding undersized fish. See pages 131–2.

Angling tackle, as with all other sports equipment, comes in a wide price range. Currently (January 1981), for around £30, it is possible to buy an efficient set of equipment for sea, trout or coarse fishing. You can pay less – but you can also pay around £180 for just a rod.

It must be assumed these days that all freshwater fishing is controlled in one way or another, and that first and foremost, you require a rod licence. These are supplied by Regional Water Authorities throughout England and Wales (see page 128). The cost varies from a few pence for a junior coarse fishing licence to £3 or £4 for a full annual trout licence.

In Scotland there are separate rules and regulations, which are mainly connected with salmon fishing. Scottish fishery laws, and the rights which various people and organisations have over different waters, are far too complicated to cover in this book. However, always assume that all fishing in Scotland, as elsewhere, is controlled. Ask locally for further details. The various River Purification Boards in Scotland are a good source of information, as are the tourist authorities, and the National Anglers' Council (see page 131).

Holding a rod licence does not, under any circumstances, mean that one can fish in any particular water. For further information about the regulations governing fishing see Chapter 13.

1 Fish Distribution

Brian Robertshaw

Rivers

Rivers can be divided into four zones or areas, each of which provides a certain limited number of species with an environment suited to their particular way of life. Rivers flowing into the sea have a fifth zone, called the estuarial zone. Although not every river or stream has all the different areas, all have one or more.

For fishing purposes these regions are named after the dominant species living in the sector. The first or uppermost tract of a stream originating in mountains or high hills is called the trout region, and is characterised by fast-running, short stretches of water, with rapids and waterfalls interspersed by deep pools of quieter water. The bottom generally consists of coarse gravel and smooth pebbles. Whilst the water temperature, even in high summer, seldom exceeds 10°C (50°F) the oxygen content is extremely high.

In addition to trout, which in these areas are usually small, wiry and non-migratory, and salmon parr, bullhead (miller's thumb), minnows and the nocturnal spined loach are frequently found. These species usually inhabit hides in the less turbulent areas behind or under stones.

The invertebrates, i.e. creatures without backbones, which are capable of surviving in this area resist being swept away in the swift current either by building a shelter attached to a stone, or by having a flattened streamlined shape, or clawed feet or suction pads to hold them in position. They consist, in the main, of caddis (sedge), stonefly and midge larvae.

The environment does not favour rooted plants, as the swift current washes away sand and soil preventing the formation of anchorage points. But several lichens, mosses, algaes and liverworts, the latter both primitive non-flowering plants, can be found growing on the boulders.

The river which has its origins in a lowland spring may have a less steep descent than one which starts on high ground, but in both types this first area must still be regarded as the trout region.

As these brooks and streams of the trout zone descend and converge, they form a water-course which is deeper and wider, somewhat warmer but still rich in oxygen. This is called the second or grayling zone.

On the river's downward journey, a change in direction, variation in gradient or the quantity of water flowing will create a variety of river beds. When the gradient is steep and the water flow is strong, the bottom is frequently composed of gravel, stones or pebbles, with little or no sand or earth particles between them, or it may be made of hard, smooth clay.

If the river bends the current on the outer side of the curve is strongest and the bottom is often 'clean', whereas the weaker flow at the inner curve allows deposits of gravel, pebbles, sand or mud to accumulate. Clean gravel can provide suitable material in which hen salmon and trout can 'dig' trenches in which they lay their eggs, whilst sand or mud will host plant life. In the grayling region, plants such as water starfoot, crowfoot and willow moss may grow in great profusion in summer months.

The less hostile environment of the grayling region encourages an increase in the variety of invertebrate fauna. Free walking caddis larvae are now more numerous, as are crustacea such as the freshwater shrimp; and where the lime content in the water is high, crayfish might be found. Molluscs such as limpets, spine shells and bladder snails also thrive, and so enrich the diet of the various fish species.

Dace, gudgeon and minnow shoal in this region, and occasionally pike or chub will be found in a section where the river suddenly deepens, creating a hole where the current is less fierce, or where there is a corner sheltered from the main current from which they can ambush unwary small fish, or snatch other morsels.

The lower limit of this region marks the end of that area which is dominated by members of the salmon family. Below this boundary they will be quickly replaced by members of the carp family, and one of these dominates and labels the next, or third zone, which is called the barbel region.

Here the water flow is still fairly rapid but in summer the water temperature may reach 20°C (68°F). Large areas of the bottom are covered with a rich mud which supports a widening variety of plants. In turn these plants provide cover for a fast expanding populace of insects and their larvae, worms and molluscs. Along the banks the vegetation becomes thicker, with plants such as rushes, reeds, plantain and arrowhead which provide shade and shelter from the main current.

The range of fish species now expands dramatically. Roach will lie and feed in streamy runs between beds of weeds, while perch, a species which moves over quite large areas, are now to be found in profusion. In quiet corners large solitary perch will often lurk waiting to seize unwary prey.

The fourth and last zone which can be truly regarded as freshwater is called the bream region. The flow is now sluggish and the water often turbid with suspended algae and fine debris. Rich in minerals carried down from the upper regions, the mud on the bottom and that which has deposited along the banks supports a luxuriant growth of weeds, for example, milfoil, hornwort, water buttercup and bistort. These in turn support a correspondingly large increase in the numbers of insects and molluscs. The slab-sided common or bronze bream, and the silver or white bream are seen, and tench find rich pickings. In quiet backwaters carp may flourish, and rudd will be active along the fringes, feeding among rush and reed stems which also provide another haunt for pike, and that other more recently introduced predatory fish, the zander (pike-perch).

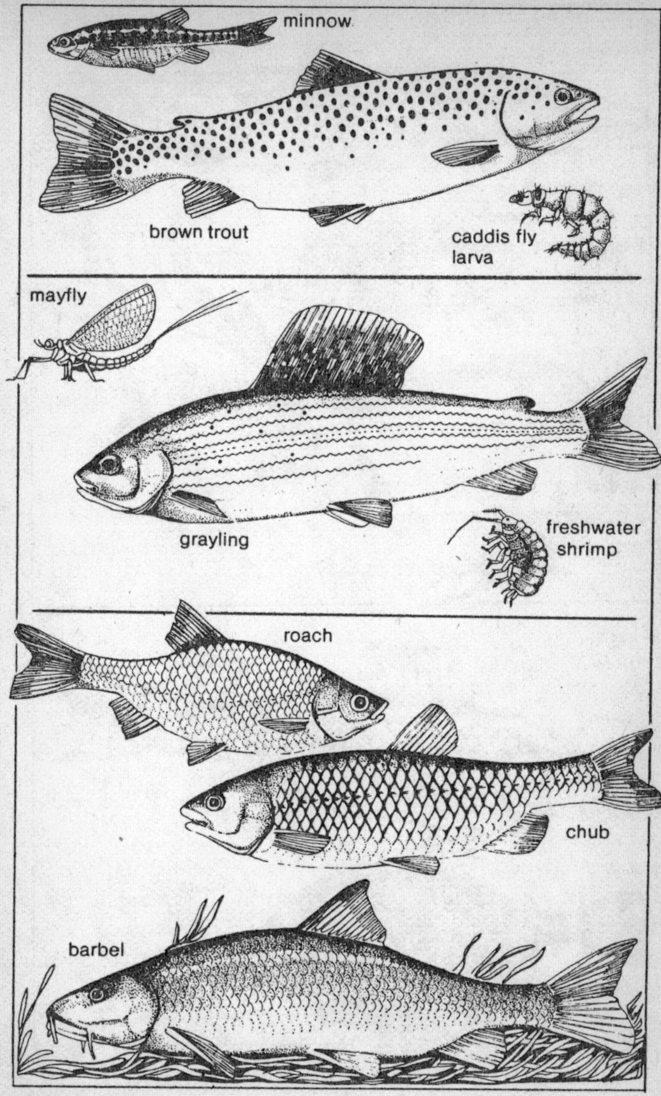

Fish and other creatures found in the trout, grayling and barbel regions of a river

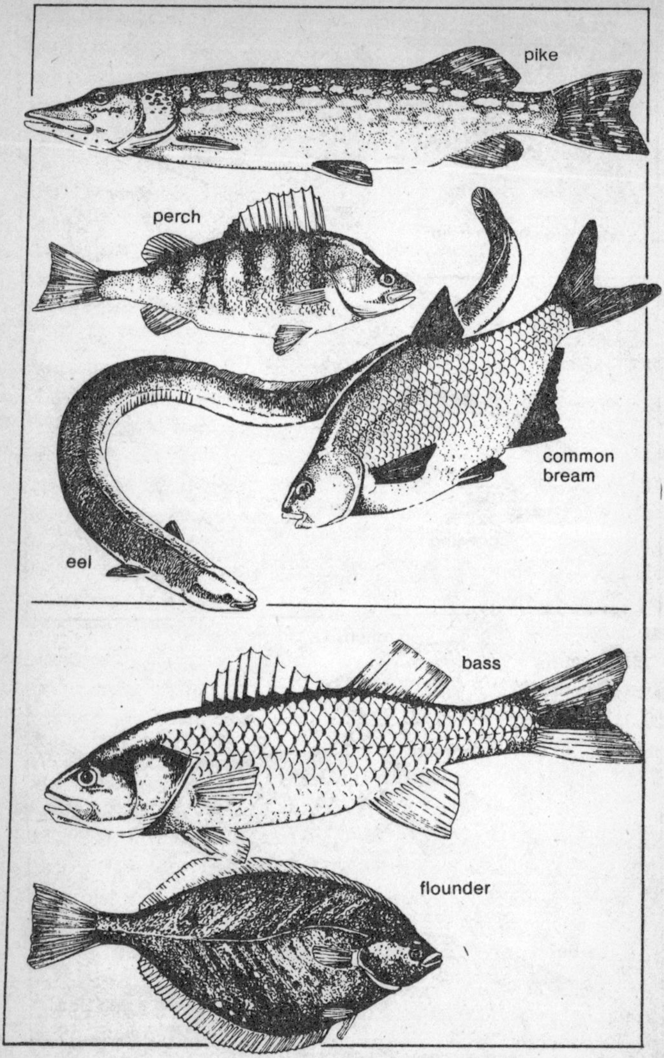

Some of the fish found in the bream region

Generally speaking this is the area where a river is teaming with life as it meanders through lush lowland water meadows. Alders, aspens and willows, which overhang the river, give shade and shelter. Each rock and hollow in the river bed and every twist and turn of the river's course gives rise to those fascinating swirls and eddies which the angler must learn to read if he is to recognise the lies in which his quarry might be found. However, in recent years some rivers have been the subject of drastic change.

Water authorities concerned with these changes have adopted the word 'canalisation' to describe what I believe to be one of the greatest follies in modern river management. Canalisation is designed to prevent flooding and does so, but, to attain this, the river is first straightened by cutting across natural curves, and then in most cases, is dredged. The banks may be raised, during which course of action trees and bankside growth are removed. Consequently the natural life of that stretch is destroyed, and the river turned into a featureless length of water. The water coming downstream is allowed to run straight to the sea, taking with it the rich mineral sediments which would, under more natural conditions, nourish both plant and animal life. There is some indication that the authorities are now recognising the damage which can be done, and developments of this kind will in future be more strictly controlled.

Occasional forays may be made into the lower parts of the bream region by fishes which truly belong to the sea. Bass, mullet and flounder, together with smelt and shad, are probably the best-known species, but they are more commonly found in the last or fifth of the river regions, namely the estuary or brackish zone.

This is an area of constant change. The ebb and flow of tides produce an action which mixes fresh and salt water. A low level of salinity can be tolerated by many freshwater fishes, as their kidneys have, within narrow limits, the ability to excrete excess body salts and so maintain an acceptable level of salt in the blood and body tissues. Migratory species have more involved excretory abilities in order to facilitate their travel from river to sea and vice versa.

These migratory species of fish are called anadromous, which means they spawn in fresh water and move to the sea to grow to maturity. They include salmon, sea trout and less commonly, sturgeon. The catadromous fish, those which spawn in the sea and return to the river or other freshwater areas to grow into adult fish, for example eel and some flounder, frequently pass backwards and forwards through the brackish zone, often pausing to accustom themselves to changes in both salinity and diet.

For all denizens of the brackish zone the food chain is now further enhanced by the appearance of prawns, shrimps, lug, and various ragworms, as well as the widening diversity of mollusc species and all the small estuarine fishes such as blenny, pout and gobies. At certain times of the year millions of elvers (small eels) arrive in the brackish zone after a journey of several thousand miles from their birthplace in the Sargasso Sea, in the Atlantic. Some of these move up-river and even cross land to colonise ponds where they feed and grow for a period which varies in individual cases from four to as many as twenty years or even more. At the end of this period the fish will answer an urge to return to its place of birth, where it will mate and die. The full story, or at least as much of it as we know, is extremely involved.

Other sea fishes ride into this area on the incoming tide, for example, and much to the delight of some London anglers, cod, whiting and sometimes a few haddock will occasionally travel some distance up the tidal section of the Thames. Evidence of the variety of fresh and salt water fish in the zone may also be seen in the assortment of fish removed from the grids covering cooling water intakes of power stations situated on the shore in estuarial zones.

Eel grass, fennel, pondweed and samphire are additions to the range of plants found, and where a rocky foothold exists, algaes such as the channelled wrack and sea lettuce may be found. Filamentous algae provide part of the diet of fish such as mullet which are often seen grazing around old piles and pier supports. Large expanses of mud flats and sandbanks in this area support a vast number of molluscs and marine worms, which in turn provide food for an expanding range of fish such as dab, sole and turbot. Buried in the soft sand or mud the venomous lesser weaver, with only eyes and bare dorsal spines exposed, lies in wait for its prey . . . and so the chain progresses. . . .

The foregoing is a much condensed description of a river and its changing pattern of life as it runs out into the sea. However, nature does not conform to strict patterns, divisions, or categories, so some rivers will vary slightly from the pattern described, but all will have some part of it in their general make-up.

Lakes and ponds

Throughout the British Isles there are numerous lakes and ponds as well as a network of canals, all of which present further complex variations of water conditions.

Lakes and ponds, dependent on size, depth and temperature, support as great a variety of plant and animal life as do the river systems. Lowland lakes and ponds are generally shallow and quite rich in nutrients; their fish life closely resembles that of the bream region of a river. Around the shore a belt of rushes and reeds, very often to a depth of 2 m (6 ft), mixes with various pond weeds, milfoil and crowfoot. Here the bream species – roach, rudd, carp and tench together with perch and pike – are found. Below the reeds, a band of water weeds may extend to a depth of 7 m (20 ft), but below this level the weeds thin quickly to reveal a muddy bottom. Plants need sun and light to thrive; deep murky water means scant plant life.

In addition to being affected by depth, life in lakes is closely related to water temperature and season. In summer, the upper layer of a body of still water is warmed by the sun. This reduces its specific gravity or 'denseness' and so this layer remains at the surface and is very rich in oxygen. Immediately below the top layer is a second section of water called the thermocline, which has a decreased oxygen content, and at the bottom is a layer of colder water which has an extremely poor oxygen content and is called the hypolimnion. In winter months the temperature throughout the lake is more uniform and the layers less pronounced – wind movement of the water helps to promote a 'mixing' action.

Lakes in the mountainous regions of Scotland, Wales and the Lake District are usually cold, deep and very poor in nutrients (oligotrophic), though well oxygenated. Although some of the species already mentioned may be found in these waters, they are frequently dominated by powan (schelly gwiniad) vendace (pollan) and trout. Because of the altitude and its related low temperatures, the effect of summer is often very limited.

Canals

The quality and quantity of life in the canal network of Great Britain varies in the extreme. Many areas are grossly polluted; others have fallen into disuse and become clogged with plants and sediment. Some canals are virtually empty, the water having leaked away into the surrounding earth leaving only shallow dirty puddles.

The stretches which have survived contain varying numbers of the cyprinid (carp) fishes, as well as perch and pike, and provide an important facility to a great number of anglers. In the Midlands, one small part of a canal which is warmed by a hot water discharge from an adjacent factory has become the home of some tropical cyclids discarded by an aquarist. Such is the diversity of life in our fresh waters.

Tackle for Coarse Fishing

Brian Watts

Tackle needed for coarse fishing can generally be grouped under two headings: basic essentials and luxury equipment.

First the basics. You will need two rods, one for each main style, float and leger fishing; a fixed spool reel with spare spools; an assortment of floats and various sizes of hook; split shot and leger weights; swimfeeders; swing, spring or quiver tips and a disgorger. Add a landing net, keep net, a tackle bag and a rod holdall to complete the set. Waterproof clothing is essential, as is suitable footwear – wellingtons with an extra pair of socks inside are probably best in winter. Finally, bait can be carried in various ways, from the northern-style maggot bag to plastic boxes of different designs.

Rods

Lightweight and economical glass-fibre three-piece ferrule-less rods with a tip action (described below) are designed for float fishing, the test curve being chosen to match the river and species of fish.

For example, a northern river such as the Tyne, which contains mainly roach and dace, can be fished with a rod having a 225-g (8-oz) test curve. Further south in the River Swale, where barbel can be caught, a rod with a 500-g (1-lb) test curve would be more appropriate. No matter where you fish, be it in the Hampshire Avon, the Thames, Ouse, or Severn, it is good angling procedure to match your equipment to both conditions and fish. Local specialist tackle dealers will always give good advice regarding such matters.

A good length of cork handle is necessary on the float rod for you will hold it most of the day. You need sufficient length to tuck under your arm to help support and balance the rod, which needs to be around 350 to 390 cm (11 to 13 ft) in length. Shorter rods restrict the depth of water which you can bottom fish. Stand-off rings, such as Bells High or Fuji, are best to keep fine line from sticking to the rod when it is wet, and a threaded end ring to take a swing or quiver tip is a useful bonus. Remember, the rod must be easy to handle for long periods even under adverse conditions.

A 'tip action' rod is one with a fast taper, and is relatively stiff or firm over much of its length. These rods offer a very fast strike action and are often referred to as being 'general purpose'. However, a range of specialist rods, similar in many respects to the general purpose rod, has been developed for match fishing. Such rods are usually long, lightweight and possess an extremely sensitive but firm action.

quiver and spring tips fitted to rods

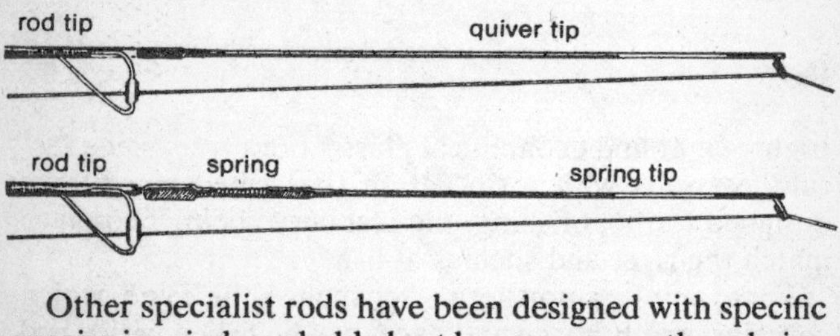

Other specialist rods have been designed with specific species in mind, probably best known among these being the large number of 'carp rods'. These have what is called 'all through action'. In other words, the taper is so designed that the rod flexes rather like a bow when it is under stress. Such rods are extremely powerful, and will cast long distances.

A leger rod is generally shorter and stronger than one designed for float fishing. The latter needs to be long to control float tackle as it travels downstream on the current; pick up line quickly as a strike is made; fish on the bottom in deep water and possibly to get out over a wide stretch of reeds along the bank. But such considerations do not apply to a leger rod. The line runs directly from tip to bait; also heavier weights are frequently part and parcel of leger fishing.

Leger rods must be fitted with a top ring which is threaded to accept a swing or quiver tip. (Some rods are built with a quiver tip as part of the top section.)

At one time brass ferrules were widely used to connect the rod sections, but today many rods are built so that one section slips into its neighbour. These rods are called ferrule-less, each section ending in a specially designed joint.

Other manufacturers build what are called spigotted ferrule-less rods. Glass spigots seldom stick like the old brass or steel ferrules, but if they should, ask somebody to help you part the sections. One should grip just above the spigot and exert a slow, very straight pull while the other twists the upper section slightly while pulling.

Rod rings wear, and when they do your line will suffer. Occasionally, take a pin and push the point through each ring in turn, revolving it slowly around the inside of the ring, noting any indentation or signs of wear. Change scored rings immediately as they tear your line which will then snap under strain.

Reels

Though centrepin reels have largely been ousted in favour of fixed spool types (see illustration), many anglers, especially those in the north, still retain one to use on 'close in' swims. Line control is perfect with this type of reel when 'trotting down' against the bank side.

However, the majority use a fixed spool reel most of the time, and it is important to set these correctly. First fill the spool with one continuous length of line (knots are a hazard), and then adjust the clutch. This can be done by holding the rod in one hand and the line end in the other. Pull in the line, and the spool should start to pay out automatically as the rod tip comes around to an angle of roughly 45° to the rod. Adjust the clutch control until the right setting is achieved. Tension should not be increased while playing a fish.

It is better to have the clutch under- rather than over-stressed. Extra braking pressure can be applied when necessary by laying a finger on the spool to check it.

Closed-face fixed spool reels are useful when casting against the wind, but generally speaking the open-face reels are preferable for leger fishing.

Reels

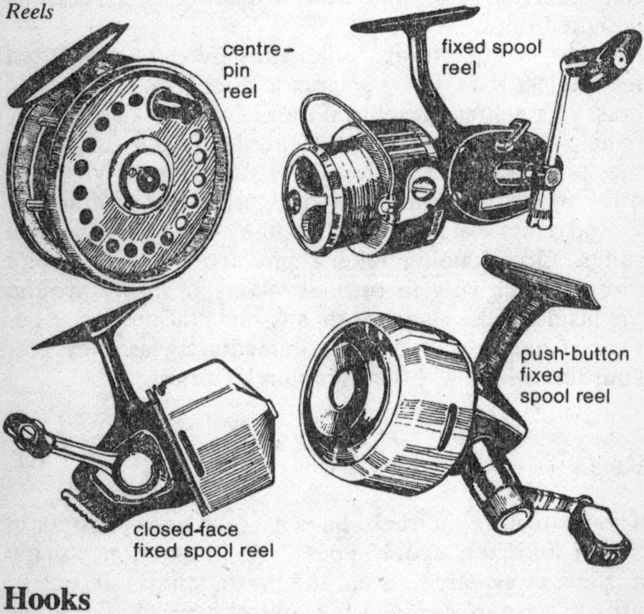

Hooks

These are the focal point of angling: the direct connection between fish and angler. Confidence in a hook is important, and once an angler finds a type he trusts, the odds are that he will stick with it. Silver, gold, blue wire, bronze? It just does not matter. In my opinion even the choice between barbed and barbless hooks is a personal

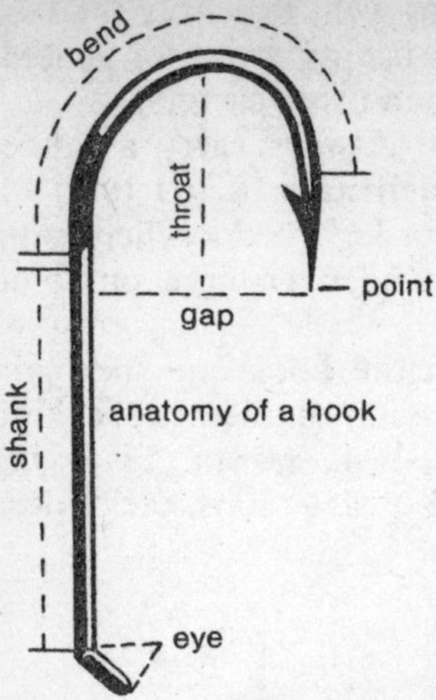
bend
throat
point
gap
shank
anatomy of a hook
eye

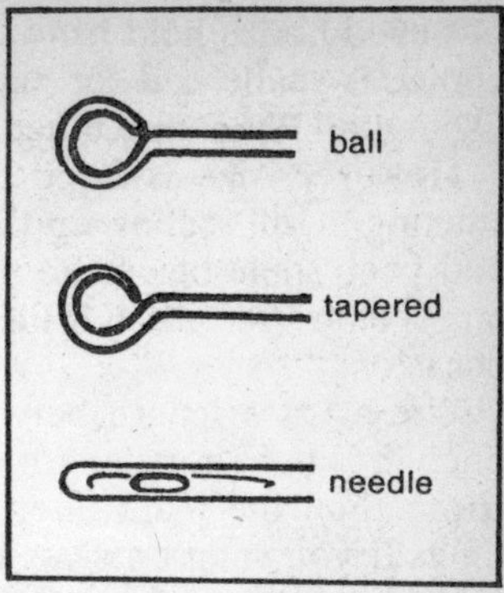
ball
tapered
needle

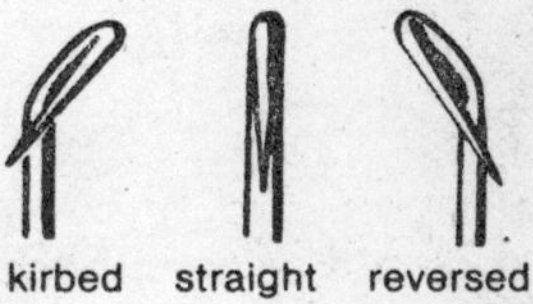
kirbed
straight
reversed

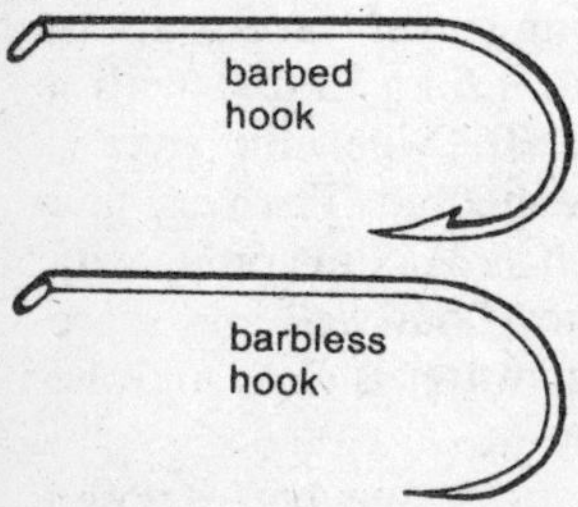
barbed
hook
barbless
hook

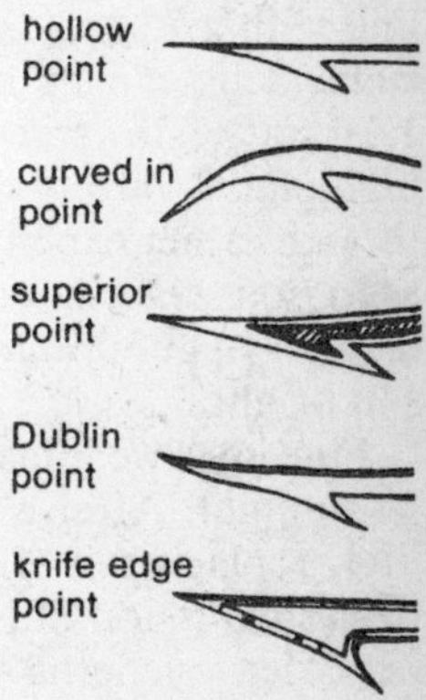
hollow
point
curved in
point
superior
point
Dublin
point
knife edge
point

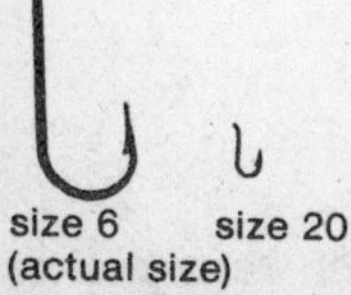
size 6
(actual size)
size 20

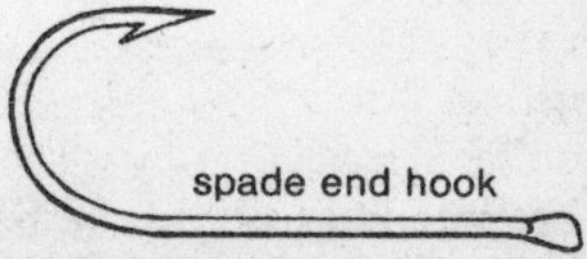
spade end hook

one. Spade-end hooks can be better concealed with bait, but eyed hooks hold fish just as well. Probably the best choice is spade-end for match fishing, eyed for general fishing, and fine wire blued when using casters.

However, size is important. Always carry a range, starting at 20, scaling up through sizes 18 and 16 to 14, and keep some bigger hooks for leger work when using large baits. A size 6 will not be over-large on some occasions.

Use a trace length between the hook and the main line. This is a short length of nylon of a lesser breaking strain than the main line, and is 45–60 cm (18–24 in) long. If you snag on river bed obstructions, tackle loss is minimal using a trace length.

Line

This is chosen with conditions and the species of fish in mind. When angling for dace and roach a 1-kg (2-lb) line with a 750-g (1½-lb) breaking strain trace is about right. This can be stepped up to 1.5 kg (3 lbs) with a 1.1-kg (2½-lb) trace for chub, or for when the river is high, and a variety of species is expected. The very fine though rather expensive lines such as Maxima or Nacrita are good when float fishing – they float well and scare fish less in good weather when the water is clear and the sun bright.

Fine lines wear fast and also deteriorate when exposed to sunlight. After a season's use, strip off and burn old line, replacing it with new. Remember that carelessly discarded nylon kills birds and other wild creatures, so never leave lengths of line lying around.

Weights

Weights are needed to hold the bait under water and to counter-balance the buoyancy of the float. Split shot should be the 'putty' or very soft type, hard shot nipped on to fine lines weakens them too much. While it is useful to carry a complete range, dust or No 6 and BB shot are often all you need.

The correct use of shot is an art, but having said that, it is also true that on some rivers shotting patterns are not as important as on others.

For example, when fishing some parts of the very wild and turbulent northern streams, such as the Tees, Wear and Tyne, shot just 30 cm (12 in) from the hook will not deter fish under normal conditions. When flood or near flood conditions exist then shot virtually next to the hook is no handicap whatsoever. However, fish in the River Swale are most 'shot shy' and so none should be placed within 45 cm (18 in) of the hook.

Similar remarks can be made regarding other streams and rivers throughout the country, reinforcing the argument that, although split shot is a small and relatively cheap item, it is enormously important, as without it, you cannot assemble float tackle for all conditions.

Other leads used by coarse anglers include those designed to hold a bait in a set position, whilst others assist the angler to fish a rolling or moving bait.

They are available in a variety of sizes. You should always carry a range of weights to suit the waters you fish, but never use a weight heavier than is needed to do the task you wish it to perform.

Floats

Wagglers, Avons, sticks, zoomers, antennae, sliders and bungs are all part of the angler's kit. A float is a device used by anglers to support a bait at a predetermined depth, and/or to give a visual indication that a fish has taken the bait.

It is important that the float chosen be not only the most efficient for the particular task, and also the smallest which will perform adequately, but that it is

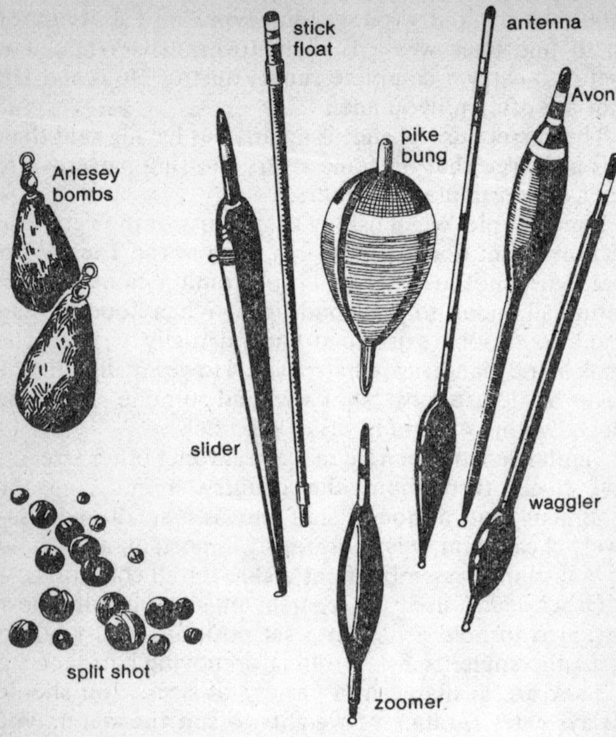

Weights and floats

carrying the right amount of weight. If a float is sitting too high in the water, its buoyancy is such that any fish taking the suspended bait will immediately feel strong resistance, and will reject the bait.

Over the years many of the problems faced by anglers have been countered by those who have designed and developed an intriguing range of floats. For example, the wagglers are ideal when the wind is blustering downstream, and, fastened to the line at the bottom only, are easy to cast without risk of tangling. However, the strike action needs a little getting used to. An Avon is usually fixed to the line top and bottom, and is useful when the wind is blowing upstream, or on still days, when stick floats are also likely to bring success. Zoomers cast well and are ideal when it is necessary to search across the river for fish. Antennae floats are wind- and wave-beaters and also are very sensitive to bites. A selection of all these types will cater for all normal requirements.

Miscellaneous items: disgorgers, tackle box, holdalls, etc.

Disgorgers are a must, for although most fish are liphooked and can often be unhooked by hand, at other times a disgorger is needed.

To avoid damaging the fish, always hold it in a wet hand or a damp cloth when removing the hook, and if using a disgorger, use a fine wire one. The kind that can be hung around your neck on a length of cord is most useful.

A tackle box and rod holdall are vital pieces of equipment. A tackle box must have strong, well-anchored straps, and a solid lid capable of taking the angler's weight so it can act as a seat. A rod holdall needs a firm base, and extra pockets for an umbrella and two banksticks.

Many swims can only be properly fished by wading but this is a practice which should only be done when in company with experienced fishermen. Waders with studded soles are best for this, but cleated soles also give a fair grip. It is best to buy a size larger than your normal shoe size, so leaving room for thick fishermen's socks to be worn over normal socks. After use always hang waders feet up. They are expensive items and can be damaged if just left lying around.

A landing net with an extending handle is particularly useful where banks are awkward and steep, and also where banks of reeds prevent a hooked fish being drawn close in. Alway use a large net, few things are more exasperating than trying to land a large fish with a small net. A fine-mesh net is best; split shot seldom snags in it, and it is kinder to the fish.

Keepnets must also be large and wide. One about 2.5 m (8 ft) long should be adequate, but once again choose one with a fine mesh. Knotted mesh nets are not allowed in some areas, for example, in the Yorkshire Water Authority region.

Other useful items are bank sticks, which are used in conjunction with keepnets and bait-box spiders, and rod rests of various designs complement certain styles of both float and leger fishing.

Using a 'magapult,' a special catapult to get maggots out to far swims to attract fish, is more efficient than hand-throwing.

Maggot bags are extremely useful when wading, not only for keeping a plentiful supply of maggots to hand, but also to hold other bits and pieces such as spare floats and hooks, and to hold the magapult. A second maggot bag can be used as a 'holdall'.

Under the heading of 'optional extras' come swing tips, spring tips, and quiver tips. These useful bite detectors screw into the threaded tip ring on match rods or leger rods, and are usually used with swim feeders. These are attachments which fit on the line above the hook and distribute maggots or groundbait in the swim around the baited hook.

An umbrella is fairly heavy, and of no earthly use whilst wading, but in winter it can be worth its weight in gold, often as a windbreak. Use a fine nylon cord for staking down the umbrella.

Polaroid sunglasses are a boon when fishing. A float can become invisible without the aid of such glasses which remove much of the reflected glare from the water.

A domestic colander can be used on the bankside to separate maggots from the sawdust in which the tackle dealer will have supplied them.

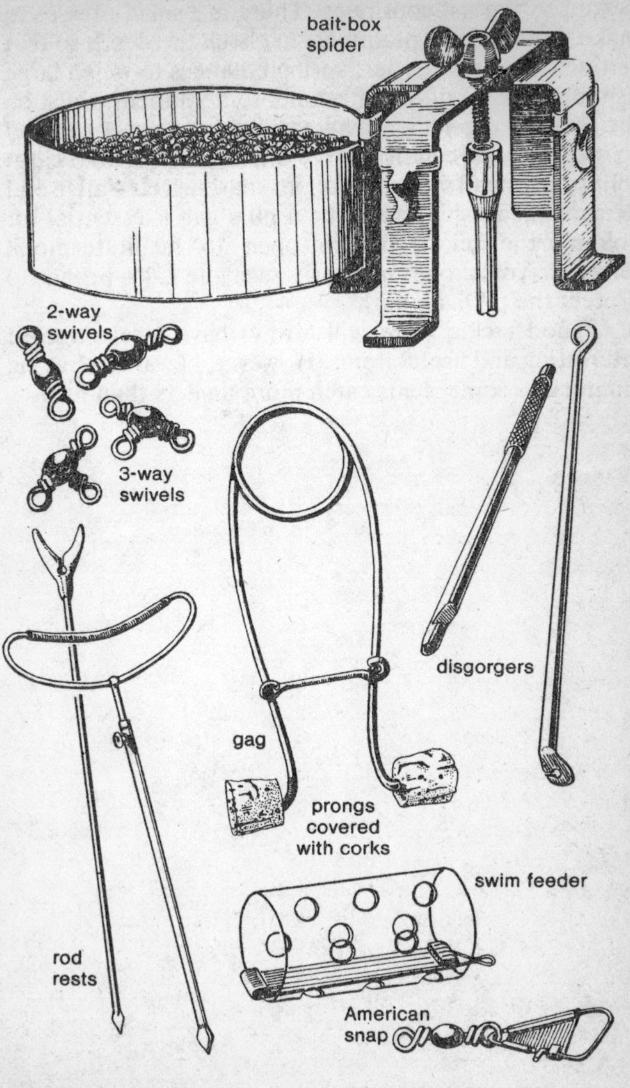

Assorted tackle

And so the list continues. There are small presses to make bread cubes; plummets to check the depth so that setting the float is easier; spring balances to weigh large fish, plus pieces of fine mesh net to hold them whilst on the scales; keepnet stretchers to hold the nets open and so create better conditions for the fish inside; float caps; split rings; small swivels; Cooper snap swivels – all useful items. When fishing for pike a pike gag is essential for holding the pike's mouth open to facilitate hook removal. You should use corks over the gag's prongs to protect the pike's mouth.

A good tackle store will always have a selection of interesting and useful items. However, beware of buying gimmicks – some items catch more anglers than fish.

3 Tackle for Trout Fishing

Richard Barder

I first started trout fishing with one rod, reel and line and it never occurred to me that there was anything wrong with this equipment. Indeed I attributed my frequent poor results to a lack of knowledge and experience. Then I went to Chew Valley Lake, a large trout reservoir near Bristol. All around me were anglers with powerful, specially designed reservoir rods. Seemingly, they and only they could reach the huge trout that rolled like porpoises thirty metres out from the bank. Defeated, I wandered off on my own. Eventually I discovered the top of a submerged bank, and by careful wading I managed to place myself thirty metres out in the lake, but by then, unfortunately, the fish had stopped rising!

Disconsolate, I waded back to the shore, my line trailing in the water behind me. Suddenly the reel began to scream, and a huge fish leaped from the water far out in the lake. I realised that I was attached to it, and when landed, it was a 2-kg (4-lb) brown trout – the biggest one caught that day.

I didn't realise it at the time, but in fact I had just learned a most important lesson; namely, by fishing in the right place at the right time, you can achieve some stupendous results, even with what some might describe as totally inadequate tackle.

However, before studying a few simple but effective trout fishing tactics, it is I feel, important to understand why fly fishing tackle is so very different to other types of angling equipment, and to know something about the seemingly complicated tackle grading system.

Probably the most fundamental difference is the fact that in both sea and coarse fishing the weight which is necessary for casting is concentrated at the end of the line, whereas in trout fishing there is virtually no weight at all in this position. Indeed, when fishing a dry (i.e. surface) fly, the principle aim is to get the fly down on to the water with no more disturbance than would be made by a midge landing on the surface.

Basically, the principle is the same whether you are casting a wet or a dry fly, the weight necessary for casting being provided by the whole line instead of just the end tackle. However, there is more to it than that; the rod must also be one specially designed for throwing not only that type of line, but also one of a particular weight.

To make it a lot easier to both understand, and also to choose matching equipment, rods and lines are given an AFTM number. These letters stand for Association of Fishing Tackle Manufacturers, the group which sets this style of grading.

The numbers run from 1 to 12 on both rods and lines, 1 being the lightest, and 12 the heaviest and most powerful.

Lines, because they are made to perform in a variety of ways, have an extra coding such as, 'WF' or 'DT'. These letters denote the type of line, 'WF' meaning weight forward, and 'DT' double tapered. As previously

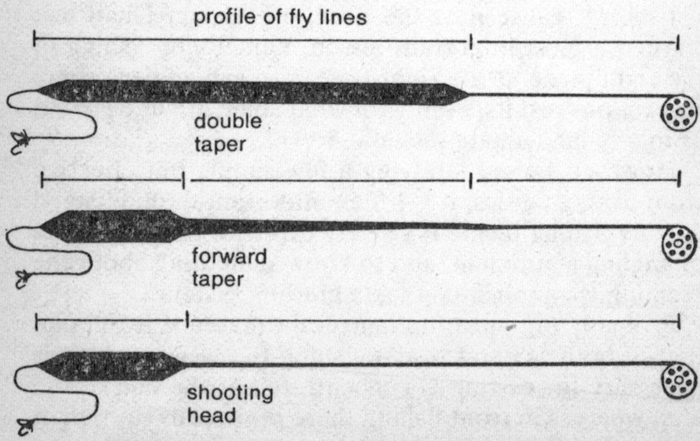

mentioned, it is the weight, plus the way in which the line has been manufactured, allied to the specially designed rod, which enables the fly to be thrown or cast.

Fly lines are also made to either float or sink, this feature is noted by adding either 'F' or 'S' to the line's classification. Put all the various codings into order and one can see how it makes sense. For example, a line carrying the following marking, AFTM 5 DTF, has been graded by the Association of Fishing Tackle Manufacturers, will be of number 5 weight, will be double tapered and will float. Here it is perhaps important to point out that the number used to indicate a fly line's weight does not in any way equate with breaking strain or test strength, two forms of grading used to show the strength of nylon line.

To match rod and line, similar numbers are put together. For example, a light rod with a 5 classification would match a line similarly coded, e.g. AFTM 5 DTF.

Reels are graded in like manner, but this is not so critical as is the relationship between rod and line.

Last but not least is the cast or leader, that all-important length of nylon between the fly and the end of the line. These can be bought as 'knotless tapered leaders', or you can tie your own. Basically, a leader is a length of nylon which continues the taper from the end of the fly line down to the fly itself. A fly line is too heavy and thick to have the fly attached to it. When presenting the fly, it could not be made to settle on the water correctly, and the fish would certainly be put off by the presence of the relatively thick line.

A leader is generally about 3 m (9 ft) long overall, and can consist of 1·2 m (4 ft) of 4·5 kg (10 lb) B.S. nylon monofilament, 0·9 m (3 ft) of 2·7 kg (6 lb) B.S., and end with 0·6 m (2 ft) of 1·36 to 1·58 kg (3 or 3½ lb) B.S. mono. This would suit a 2·4- to 2·7-m (8- to 9-ft) rod, but a leader of about 2 m (7 ft) would be more appropriate when fishing with a shorter rod, or casting on a small stream or brook.

When using a very small fly, a 0·9- or 1·1-kg (2- or

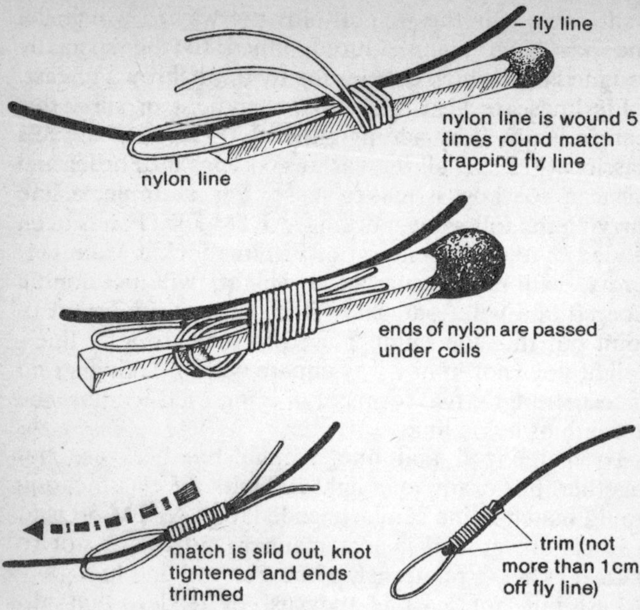

Making a permanent loop at each end of the fly line

2½-lb) B.S. mono would be more suitable for the final 0·6 m (2 ft) of the leader.

There are no hard and fast rules governing either the overall length or the actual strength of the different nylons used to make a 'self tied' leader. Some prefer to start with a 5·4 kg (12 lb) or even 6·8 kg (15 lb) B.S. mono; these are niceties which your own experience plus knowledge which you glean from others will enable you to settle to your own satisfaction.

Apart from the basic rod, line and reel (one with two spools, the first loaded with a floating and the other with a sinking line), the fly fisherman needs little else. Just a selection of flies, plus a bottle of waterproofing liquid to ensure the flies float, a spring balance, a few ready-made casts (or the nylon to make them), a disgorger, a priest, and a bag to put it all into, and believe it or not, you can fish for a season perfectly well.

In fact, following a move from one house to another, with virtually my entire collection of tackle hidden in packing cases, all I had to hand was an inexpensive 2·7-m (8½-ft) glass-fibre rod, a landing net, plus a bag of small items of tackle, including two reels. Both were 95 mm (3¾ in) diameter, one was loaded with a 6 DTF line, the other a 6 DTS line. Fortunately, the rod was designed to throw a 6 line, and this tackle was adequate for me to be able to fish successfully in the Kennet, Lambourn and Enborne. While using a dry fly, I caught a couple of 1·3-kg (3-lb) fish; and using wet flies, nymphs and lures, I caught many more fish from a wide variety of lakes, gravel pits and reservoirs. I fished for the entire season with what might be fairly described as 'minimal tackle,' and my end of season total was higher than usual.

A rod weight of 6 or 7 will handle most trout fishing situations perfectly well. Heavier lines, such as weight 9, which are used with powerful reservoir rods, are good for distance casting when fishing large waters, but such lines land far too heavily on the water to be successful when fishing an average stream or river.

In my opening remarks I mentioned the importance of fishing in the right place at the right time. Equally vital is a working knowledge of the trout's habits, and the facility to chose a fly suited to the occasion.

Although studying the trout can reasonably be described as an occupation for a lifetime, you can learn a lot by listening to other, more experienced anglers, reading, and by taking time to just look at what is going on all around you, both below and on the surface.

Clear water, a pair of polarised glasses, patience and the ability to absorb and understand what you see will help enormously. The knowledge which you will surely acquire as a result of observation, reading and general fishing experience will help you to make fairly accurate decisions regarding the fly or nymph you should try at any particular time.

However, before that day arrives, it is best to ask for advice regarding 'local favourites'. Your tackle dealer, water bailiff or other anglers will surely help, but in all probability a few of the patterns described in Chapter 11 will enable you to fish with a fair chance of success.

For a start you might keep your flies on a lambswool pad, or a piece of felt. Naturally, a custom-built fly box is the best, but never jumble a selection together in an old tin box, the hook points will suffer; and so will the hackles, wings and so on.

4 Tackle for Sea Angling

Alan Wrangles

Shore-fishing rods

Hollow glass beach-casting rods are still the most widely used although an increasing number nowadays are made from a mixture of carbon and glassfibre.

The 'hollow' type of rod offers the best 'action' for casting the tackle and baits associated with shore fishing. 'Action' is the term used to describe the way in which a rod (any rod) reacts to the strain of casting or playing a fish. Various factors combine to give a rod its action. These include the material used to build it, the method employed to join the sections when the rod is assembled, and the overall shape, which is determined by the designer. For example, the rod may taper continuously from butt to tip, or it may have what is called a 'reverse taper'. The former can give a very fast tip action and some rods of this type are particularly suited to a casting system known as the South African. In this style the bait is brought around in a sweeping movement which carries the terminal tackle in an arc almost parallel with the ground. The disadvantage of this style can be seen if we consider what might happen if the cast is inefficiently operated, or if the line snaps. It is possible for the lead and baited hook or hooks to fly at body height along the shore, and a 100-g (4-oz) lead with a pointed end, travelling at perhaps 130 km/h (80 mph) is a potentially lethal object.

A reverse taper rod has a softer, but powerful bow-like action, and if used in conjunction with the very popular 'lay-back' casting style, is much less of a potential danger to those near by, should the end tackle break away, or 'crack off' as it is called.

When it comes to actually selecting a rod for your own use, there are various factors to consider. Your local angling conditions, that is, the circumstances which exist where you will be fishing, set certain parameters, and so to an extent the choice is narrowed automatically. For example, where tidal conditions force the use of, say, 170- to 225-g (6- to 8-oz) weights, then it is essential that not only must the rod be capable of casting these weights, but the line must also be of matching strength. It then follows that the reel must be both large and strong enough to carry the amount of the type of line it will need to hold, and also perform adequately when under strain.

Briefly, all the main items of tackle – rod, reel and line – must be matched, for if they are out of balance, the power of one component can overwhelm the other two, and the result will be either tackle failure, or an inability to fish correctly. These facts apply equally to all types of fishing tackle.

Having settled on the basic type of rod you need, then make sure that it suits your height and build by checking the hand grips and the positioning of the reel fittings. Having to over-stretch to hold the rod, or for that matter feeling cramped whilst using it will have a detrimental effect on your casting. It really is essential that you feel comfortable, and that you are able to control the equipment throughout the casting sequence.

Beach casting rods are normally about 300 to 360 cm (10 to 12 ft) long, and hand grips vary from short plastic ones with moulded finger grips to long rounded cork handles. Which you select is a matter of personal choice – just make sure that it is comfortable, that the reel fits correctly, and that there is still room for adjustment when it is fixed tightly to the rod, as some wear and 'settling-in' is bound to occur.

Shore-fishing reels

Most beach anglers use either a fixed spool or an orthodox multiplying reel. Given similar conditions,

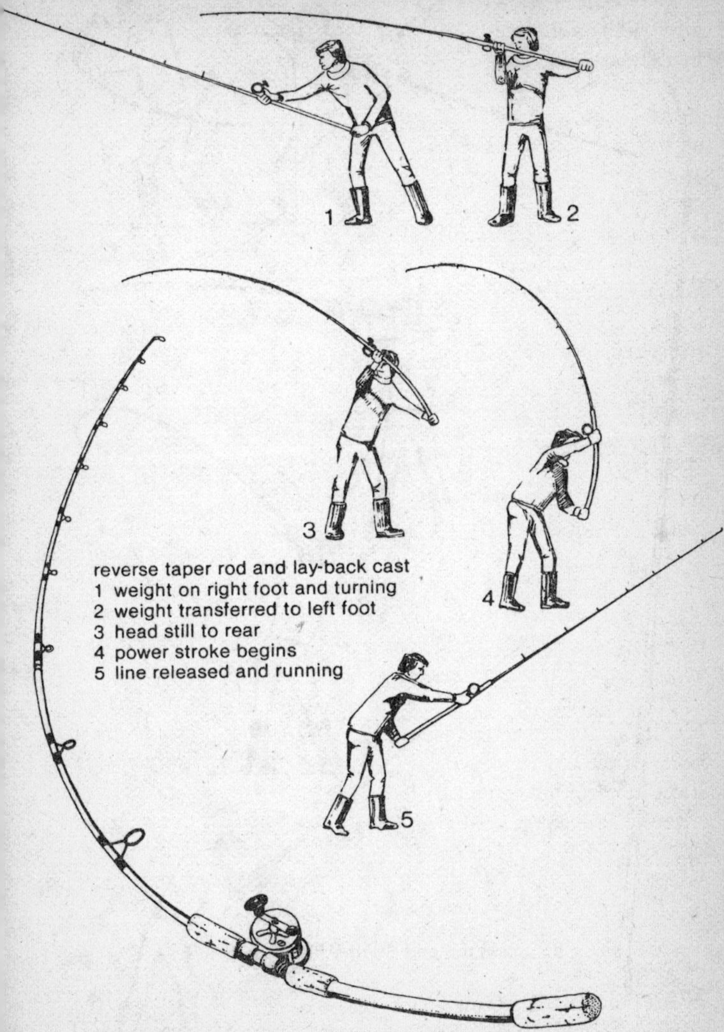

reverse taper rod and lay-back cast
1 weight on right foot and turning
2 weight transferred to left foot
3 head still to rear
4 power stroke begins
5 line released and running

tip action rod and South African cast

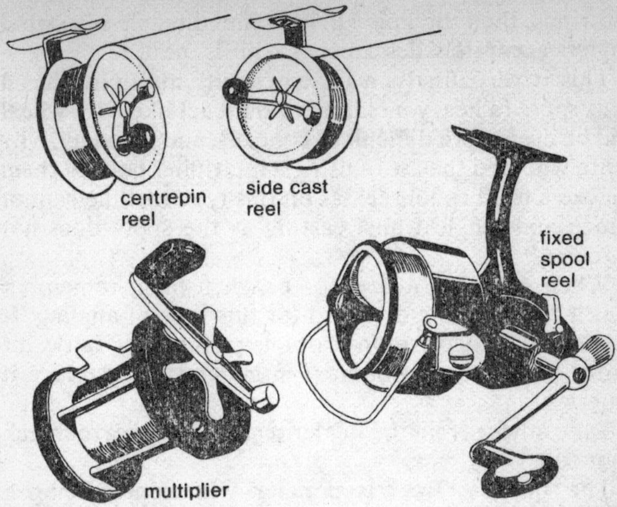

Reels

such as line thickness, type of rod, etc., the revolving spool multiplier will outcast its rival. However, this basic fact does not take human aptitudes into consideration.

A multiplier is a more complicated reel to use, and despite the many and varied controls fitted by different manufacturers designed to eliminate or at least restrict the possibility of the spool over-running, this still happens, and some anglers never really master the art of using this type of reel.

The act of casting sends the tackle on its seaward flight. As the cast is made, the rod is forced into an arc, and, put as simply as possible, as your hands reach their final position, the rod is still bent, and the tackle swinging at an ever-increasing speed.

As the rod straightens, giving the end tackle the last powerful urge, the line is released. In turn, this force sets the spool spinning. If the spool throws off line more rapidly than the flighting tackle can draw it through the rod rings, then the line will bunch and tangle into what anglers accurately describe as a 'birds' nest'.

This is why, firstly, a beach-casting multiplier has a light spool (a heavy metal one would act like a fly-wheel and be even more difficult to control), and secondly, why those who find the art of using a multiplier beyond them choose a fixed spool reel, as on this type the line cannot bunch and tangle whilst casting as the spool does not revolve.

When choosing a reel for beach fishing, remember that it must be one designed for this type of angling. It needs to be as corrosion proof as possible, as saltwater and the marine environment in general will damage it otherwise.

Take advice from the dealer regarding a reel to match your rod.

The side cast reel is popular with some, being a curious mixture of both fixed and revolving spool reels, but it does not have a geared drive.

Shore-fishing line

Nylon monofilament (i.e. single-strand) line is in general use for beach fishing. It is the only type of line which works satisfactorily with a fixed spool reel. If you attempted to check a rapidly revolving multiplier spool that was loaded with a multi-strand braided line, you would strip the skin from your thumb. Braided line is also too bulky for beach fishing.

All the well-known brands of line are good, but some anglers prefer a mono line which has slightly more 'spring' than another – conversely, there are those who choose a line which is as limp as possible. It is very much a personal choice; I like a line which is as thin as possible for a given strength.

Line is graded according to its breaking strain (B.S.) or test strength. A line having, for example, a 13·5-kg (30-lb) B.S. should not snap until a steady strain exceeding 13·5 kg (30 lb) has been placed on it. However, a line with a 13·5-kg (30-lb) test strength will break as the strain almost reaches 13·5 kg (30 lb). Such a line will not stand up to any pull in excess of its rated strength.

It must be remembered that nylon mono line stretches, and so if it has been excessively strained, it should be taken off the reel and left to 'recover' for an hour or so. Stretched nylon line can ruin a metal spool by crushing and so distorting it, therefore never leave line in a stretched condition on a reel of any type.

Booms, swivels, buckles, etc.

These various items of 'wire-work' are essential when assembling different tackle arrangements or 'rigs'. Never use more pieces of metal than absolutely necessary, and make sure they are not too large, as unlike line, swivels and buckles do not carry a strength rating. With experience your eyes will tell you if the rig looks wrong.

Always keep them free from corrosion; this can fray the line and also prevent a swivel from working correctly.

Leads

The various shapes and sizes have been developed to complement the different styles of angling, as well as the many constantly changing conditions.

A bomb-shaped lead is basically the most efficient for casting, the weight being concentrated in its base and preventing it from tumbling end over end whilst it is flying through the air. This reduces the risk of the end tackle becoming tangled and not working correctly when it settles on the sea bed.

However, conditions do not always allow such a lead to be used, and a compromise has to be found among one of the many other shapes available.

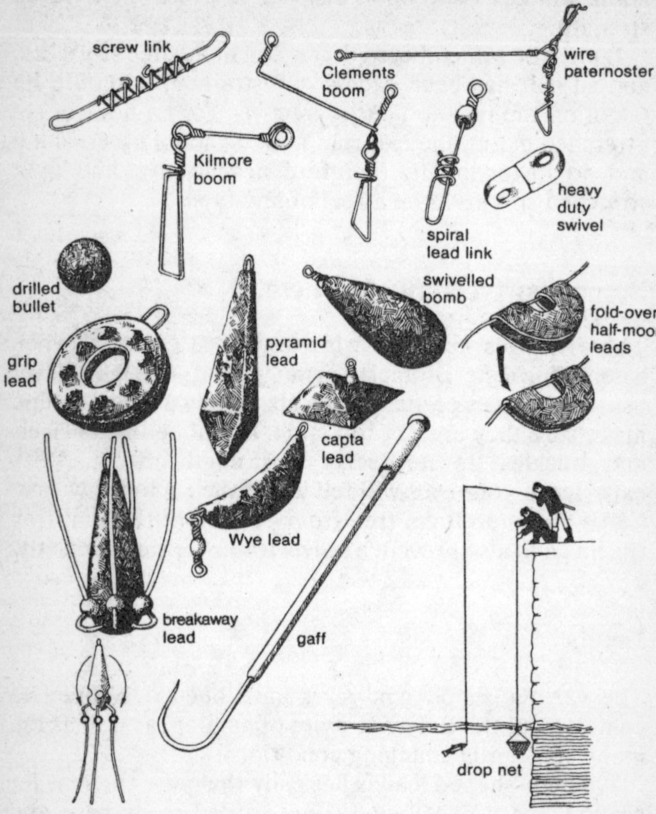

'Wirework', leads and other equipment

Accessories

Apart from all the obvious angling accessories, ranging from a woolly hat and wellington boots to a pack or box to store and carry the many small pieces of equipment, there are those very important items which are used to land what you have caught.

Although perhaps the majority of the fish you hook can be reeled straight up without any problems, inevitably, sooner or later, you will hook one that needs special treatment.

Always consider how you are going to land that which you might catch. It is pointless to cast from a spot where you would find it either impossible or personally dangerous to attempt landing a big fish. Every year people die in situations such as this.

A rod is not designed to be used as a crane, and in any case, a fish of reasonable size would probably tear free as soon as its total weight was placed on the hook. So landing a sizable fish means using either a net or a gaff. A drop net is used when fishing from a pier, a landing net when boat fishing, and a gaff can be used from either a boat or a beach. You should only gaff fish you are going to kill, as the gaff damages them, and is likely to subject them to a slow death from disease.

Never chase the fish with a net or gaff; sink the net's rim, draw the fish over the net and then lift quickly. In similar fashion, draw the fish to the gaff, and pull the fish clear in a single and continuous sweep.

Boat-fishing rods

These are shorter than those used for shore fishing, usually between approximately 180 and 210 cm, (6 to 7 ft) and often manufacturers describe them as being in a particular 'class'.

A 13·5-kg (30-lb) class rod is built to match a 13·5-kg (30-lb) test or 13·5-kg (30-lb) B.S. line; there are also, for example, 9-kg (20-lb), 18-kg (40-lb), 22·5-kg (50-lb) and 36-kg (80-lb) classes.

As ever, price dictates quality. The cheaper solid glass rods are tough and serviceable, but not as pleasurable to use as the more expensive kinds. When under strain, the line should always pass from ring to ring, and follow the rod's curve, never dropping beneath it.

Boat-fishing reels

Spools should be large and strong, and preferably made of metal. Their gear ratio is often lower than that used in beach-fishing reels where a fast retrieve through the surf can be advantageous. However, as here we are mainly concerned with estuarial and inshore fishing, where conditions are generally less demanding than those which are encountered over deep off-shore marks, really heavy duty reels are beyond the scope of this section.

Remember the basic features which are needed for efficient boat angling, and buy a reel matched to your rod.

Boat-fishing line

Nylon monofilament line is normally perfectly adequate for most inshore boat fishing requirements. Braided line is often used in deep water where heavy leads and line stretch can make hooking a fish difficult, but these are not problems associated with inshore and estuarial boat angling for species such as mullet, flounder, plaice, bream, whiting, etc.

5 Coarse Fishing Baits

Brian Watts

Almost anything the angler can eat, plus many items that he can't, can be used as hook or loose-feed bait for coarse angling. However, always remember that matching a suitable groundbait or loose feed with the hookbait helps to attract fish and keep them feeding. Groundbait is thrown into the water to attract fish to a baited hook – maggots used for this purpose are called 'loose feed'.

The basic breadcrumb type of groundbait, available at all fishing tackle shops 'by the pound' is the ideal base, but other ingredients can be added to it to increase its attraction. Various types or flake or dehydrated potato are popular, as is pollard, a fine bran containing some flour, which can also be used on its own. It provides a relatively cheap bulk groundbait, but it can only be used when fishing close in as it breaks up if you try to throw it far. In fast-running water it disperses quickly.

Adding oils to groundbait seldom has much effect. The best is aniseed oil, available from chemists, which occasionally does seem to bring fish into the swim – and also move other anglers away!

Maggots

Maggots are by far the most popular bait. They are easily obtained and will attract every species of fish, with the possible exception of stone loach! They are good loose feed, and can also be mixed into other groundbait. Always keep them in clean sawdust to prevent them sweating, and in containers which provide ventilation. In a sealed container such as a plastic bag they will soon die.

In their natural state maggots are white with a black

'bauble' inside which can be seen to move up and down the body as they wriggle. Special foods can be introduced into their diet to give them colour, and it is possible to dye them yourself with a little care. Maggots treated in this way can be more attractive as bait. An ideal colour is yellow (or bronze) and annato- (a colouring agent) fed maggots which are this colour are excellent for fast northern streams.

Dye comes in powder forms, usually in small tubes, and is available from most tackle shops. For a deep yellow colour, ask for the 'chrysodine' dye. You require a large jar with a lid and the maggots must be clear of all sawdust before they are ready to colour.

Clean the jar, and add a small amount of cold water to a depth of 0·5 cm (¼ in) and mix sufficient dye to create a deep colour. Tip the maggots in, not too many at a time, just enough for some to get above the liquid by climbing on each other. Replace the lid, which should be perforated, and allow the maggots to work in the liquid until they are well coloured.

Ten minutes may be enough, depending on the strength of the mix. Scrape the maggots out in a mass, let them fall into a small amount of sawdust in which they can dry out, and also remove any excess dye as they wriggle. Finally, place them into fresh dry sawdust in which they can be kept ready for use.

White maggots benefit from softening and cleaning in a flour mix overnight before use.

During the winter, a few maggots which are for hookbait only should be kept in a tin inside a warm pocket. The warmth provides active 'wriggly' baits. Other maggots left in the container on the bankside soon go semi-dormant in the cold.

Hot weather, and particularly direct sunlight has a lethal effect on maggots; they will soon stretch and die if left in a container with the sun shining directly on to it. If you leave your supply on the bank, place the container in the shadow of a bush or tree, and leave its lid off so that they do not sweat.

Usually from 0·5 to 1 litre (1 to 2 pints) of maggots are needed for a day's fishing.

Casters

As the maggot's skin hardens into a shell and it forms a chrysalis, it becomes what anglers call a caster. Casters should sink, and they are an ideal clear-water and summer bait. Fished on a fine wire hook, which penetrates the shell without bursting it open, casters were for several years a top fish-taking bait, not only on the rivers Swale and Tees, but on many others as well. Currently, the maggot has made a comeback, but casters still often account for better quality fish.

Many anglers place their supply of casters into a pan or pail of water before using them. Any that float they discard. However, when an air bubble forms inside the chrysalis, which is what causes them to float, they can still be used for specific purposes. For example, a few can be thrown into the river, and as fish rise to take them, you can spot where they are lying, and adjust your tactics accordingly. Do not throw too many in, as you will only encourage the fish to follow them downstream!

During the summer when fish are basking in shallow swims, floating casters make an enticing hookbait. Use one, on an unshotted trace, about 40 cm (2 ft) below the float.

If, when checking your casters you find that virtually all of them are floating, they can be 'persuaded' to sink by bringing them to the boil, very slowly, using an old pan which can be kept for such jobs. Casters treated in this way will not keep, they must be used the same day.

Worms

Worms are a deadly bait, and if they could be obtained in the same quantities as maggots they would soon become the top hookbait. Even without being available in the quantity to allow loose feeding your swim, they still take many fish. Brandlings, the yellow- and red-banded variety which thrive in manure, are particularly good when fishing for species such as grayling and perch. Both will take brandling on days when maggots are ignored.

Small red worms often tempt big roach, and on a river which I fish a lot, the Tyne, they can be a real killer when fished in conjunction with maggots used as loose feed.

If you have a spare couple of metres of garden try breeding your own worms. A 15-cm (6-in) layer of manure covered with a thick piece of matting which is kept damp will ensure a constant supply. You might be able to buy a small supply of brandlings from the tackle shop to start the 'farm' off. Worms are a very important bait when the rivers are up and carrying a lot of colour.

Wasp grubs

Wasp grubs, another excellent bait, are difficult to obtain and virtually impossible to buy. It is both difficult and dangerous to attempt killing the active wasps and then opening the nest to obtain the grubs. However, if you should know anyone who is having a nest removed by professional operators, and it is possible for you to obtain some comb, do so, as the grubs are well worth having. In, or on the comb there may well be dead or dying wasps, so take great care; if they are at all active, back away.

The interior of the nest can be kept in a deep freeze for future use. The combs make excellent groundbait, and can even be used on the hook. But no matter how good this bait may be, it is not worth getting stung for.

In the future, two baits just coming on to the market could soon prove extremely popular, and just as deadly as wasp grubs. Expensive, true, but bee and moth grubs,

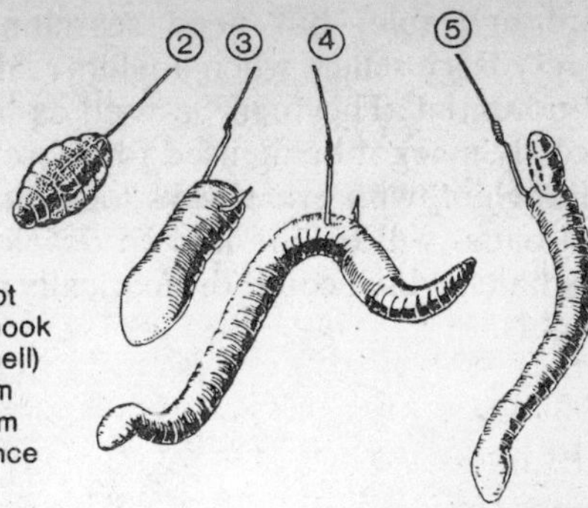

1. double maggot
2. caster (note hook filling out bait shell)
3. tail of lobworm
4. whole lobworm (hook is ⅓ distance from head)
5. caster and worm (caster covers hook tip)

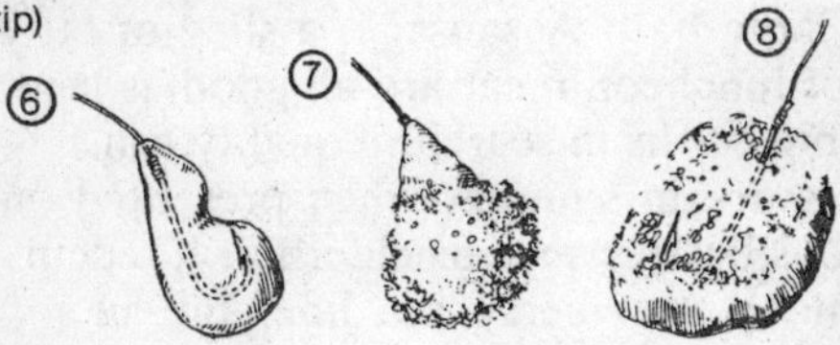

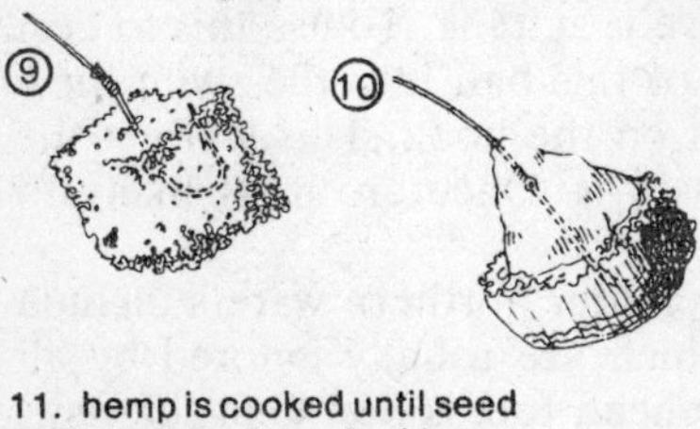

6. bread paste (it can be an advantage to indent bait above hook point)
7. bread flake
8. crust with hook tip just showing
9. bread cube with hook tip just showing
10. platform of crust with bread paste covering hook shank (crust adds buoyancy to heavy paste)

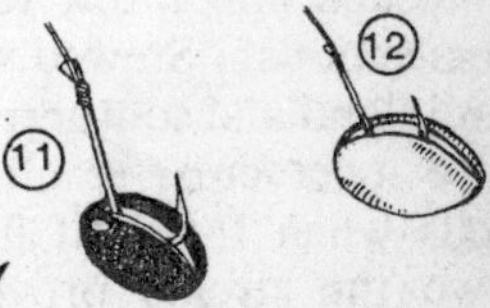

11. hemp is cooked until seed splits and hook pushed into split
12. wheat
13. parboiled potato

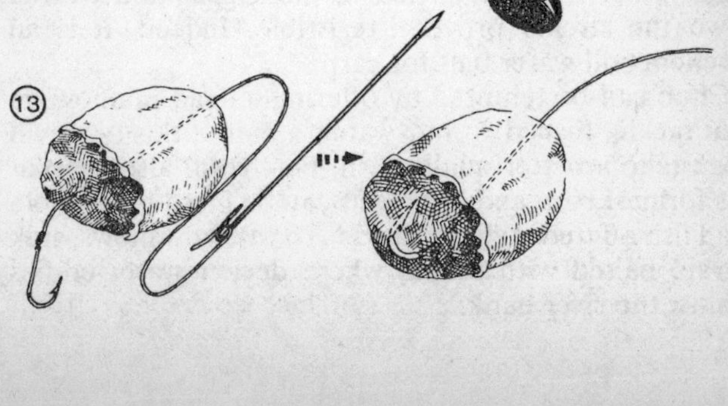

which are available, but need searching for, could become very large sellers when anglers realise their fish-catching potential. They can be used as hookbait with the less costly maggot being used for loose feeding.

Match anglers, who are always looking for new and successful baits, will be the first to develop the use of these new baits, which could dramatically increase their catch weights.

'Food' baits

The bigger species, for example barbel and chub, frequently like a large bait. A sausage, a slice of fatty bacon or a cube of luncheon meat are all good as leger baits when using big hooks in search of quality fish.

Fruit baits can score in summer when presented on float tackle. Various berries such as elderberry, redcurrant, blackcurrant or strawberry are fine, but in my opinion the most effective is sultana. To use this to best effect, loose feed some of this bait into the swim for a few days before using it on the hook. This will get the fish to show an interest in it. Dace are most likely to respond.

Baits to avoid on the colder northern waters include hempseed and tares, which are usually ignored by all species of fish. Stewed wheat, too, is best kept for visits to midland and southern rivers, but sweet corn can bring quite spectacular results. Both grayling and chub have spells when this bait fished on float gear and trotted down the stream proves irresistible. Indeed, it is an excellent still water bait for carp.

Chub can be tempted by offering a dead minnow on float tackle. Fished at mid-water, a bait of this type will often take a better quality fish. Perch will also snap at this form of bait, and large eels can be lured by a whole dead fish offered on leger tackle. To catch minnows, sink a trap, baited with bread, where deeper water eddies against the river bank.

Soft cheese is a well-proven bait, and it can be fished on float or leger tackle and will catch roach and chub, though dace and eels sometimes go for it as well.

Bread used either as paste or flake is another traditional bait which has accounted for many of the big match weights from the River Tees when chub have been the quarry. Leger gear is often used in conjunction with a big hook and large matching bait.

Of all the bread baits, the one with the strongest texture, and therefore best for long distance casting, is crust. This can be either irregularly shaped pieces pulled from a loaf or squares cut and trimmed with a knife. When fishing with bread, remember to 'strike' or lift the rod tip before reeling in. This action will jerk the bait from the hook and so provide an amount of groundbait. When using any sort of paste bait make sure the hook point is exposed so that it will drive home as a strike is made.

Several artificial baits are available in tackle shops, artificial maggots and minnows are two good examples. By all means keep a selection in your tackle box, but for emergency use only.

It is always worth noting what local competition reports say about baits. Use these as an indicator to the type of bait you should take with you, but no matter what the current 'in' bait happens to be, never go fishing without a good supply of the best maggots you can buy. These are probably the best 'all round' bait you can use.

6 Flies and Lures

Richard Barder

When I caught a big rainbow trout in Kenya I was using a fly called the Mrs Simpson, and I was told by one of the leading local anglers that it imitated a small crayfish-like creature of which the local trout were very fond. I caught a number of other trout using the Mrs Simpson, but I never had even the suspicion of a take using the flies I had brought out from England. As usual, local knowledge was best!

It is very important to use flies that imitate or give the impression that they are food for the trout. However, I expect you have noticed that some of the most successful lake flies, or, more correctly, the lures, imitate nothing that any English-born trout has ever eaten. It is believed that these flies and lures are taken out of curiosity or because they stimulate the trout's attack mechanism, but I have a private theory that some successful monstrosities are taken by the trout in sheer self defence!

At this point I want to make a distinction. Native-born brown trout are far less susceptible to non-imitative flies and lures than rainbows, which are farm-bred descendants of a North American race of trout. A brown trout can be stimulated, or induced, to take a fly that reminds him of the fry of some fish with which he is familiar. He is less likely to take it if it doesn't remind him of any such fish. The same applies to flies that imitate aquatic flies.

It is obviously useful to have some knowledge relating to aquatic flies that interest trout, and I cannot emphasise too strongly that entomology is not a dirty word! An hour spent studying the simple guidelines I gave in my book *Dry-Fly Trouting for Beginners* will pay enormous dividends in terms of fish caught.

Broadly speaking, natural flies found in or around water are of two kinds. Type one starts life underwater as eggs, which eventually hatch out and make their way to the surface. Type two are land flies that fall, have been blown, or have some interest of their own in making their way on to the water. Among the first type, March Browns, Olives, Iron Blues, Blue-winged Olives, Pale Wateries, Mayflies and Sedges are all important. In the second category, Black Gnats and Hawthorn fly are important. Personally I never carry either of the latter, but a friend of mine catches plenty of fish on a Black Gnat.

There are hundreds of different imitations of the flies I have mentioned, but you will catch as many or even more fish than the next man if you buy some March Browns to imitate the March Browns; Kites Imperials, Medium Olives and Ginger Quills to imitate the Olives; Orange Quills for the Blue-winged Olives; Ginger Quills again for the Pale Wateries; Grey Wullfs for the

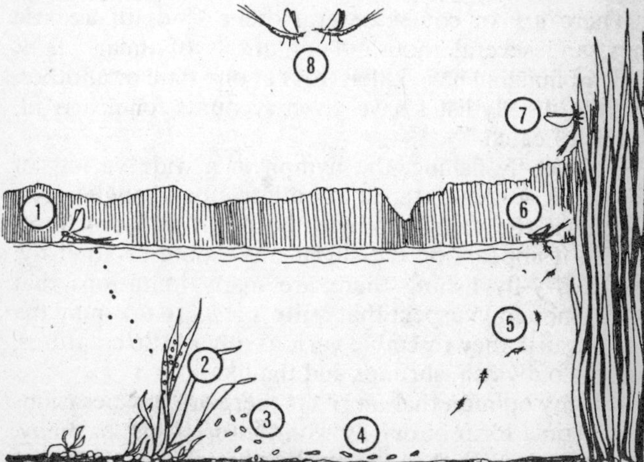

The life cycle of an aquatic fly: 1 eggs laid on surface of water; 2 eggs submerge and some stick to vegetation; 3 some eggs drift to the bottom and sink in the mud; 4 eggs change to larvae; 5 larvae become nymphs; 6 immature adult fly lives on surface; 7 when fully grown leaves water . . . 8 . . . and mates to start the cycle again.

Mayflies; and Cinnamon Sedges for the Sedges. Add to taste some Black Gnats and Hawthorn flies and you are in the dry-fly business. Sizes should be 14s and 16s, except for the Sedges and Mayflies which can be 10s and 12s, and the March Browns which should be 12s.

Trout seem to have a great liking for those water-based flies which leave the surface of the water to mate, and then come back to the river to lay their eggs, and eventually collapse and die on the surface. When it reaches the collapsing stage the fly is called a spinner, and when it is dead it is called a spent spinner. It is worth knowing that a Pheasant Tail is a good imitation of the spinners of several of the Olives, Iron Blues, Blue-winged Olives and Pale Wateries, and is therefore a useful fly if in doubt! I would be perfectly happy to dry-fly fish using only Ginger Quills, Pheasant Tails, Lunn's Particulars (a favourite spent pattern), Kites Imperials, Grey Wullfs and Cinnamon Sedges.

There are of course several other kinds of aquatic flies, and several thousand imitations of them, all of which I imagine have killed trout at one time or another, but the dry-fly list I have given accounts for nearly all the fish I catch.

For wet-fly fishing, the nymph of a wide variety of species is of great interest to both trout and angler. The nymph is the name given to the fly in its larval form before it appears on the surface as a dun, or adult fly. As in dry-fly fishing there are many imitations that work, though I suspect that quite a few are taken by the fish because they resemble various other little creatures, such as baby fish, shrimps and the like.

It is my opinion that on rivers there are few occasions when some form of dry fly won't interest just as many, or even more fish than the wet fly, though I concede that there are moments when a nymph is useful.

In still waters it's a different ball game. The bottom feed is often very rich, particularly in reservoirs, and the trout don't have their feed brought to them by the current. Not surprisingly they wander about, and as

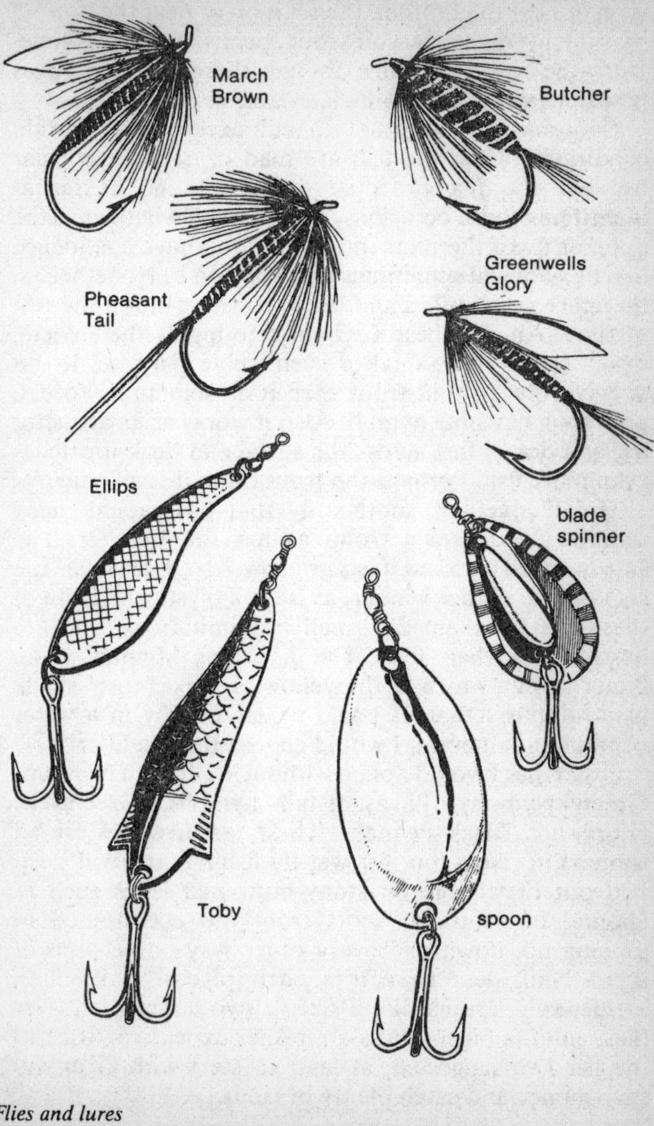

Flies and lures

most of the hatching, crawling and other insect activity is on or near the bottom, then it is on or near the bottom that the average reservoir trout spends most of its time. Here the wet fly is king, though there are sometimes occasions when the dry fly is useful.

Choosing wet flies is not difficult except under certain conditions, when the fish are mad on some particular fly. Far too many people don't even go as far as identifying those occasions, they just use whatever is the popular fly of the moment. And if you have confidence in a fly, you will sometimes catch fish on it! Nonetheless, there are certain flies and lures that have stood the test of time. Among these I would rate highly the Invicta, which seems to be dual or even treble purpose. It is a deceiver fly, in that trout take it as something to eat, perhaps a hatching nymph. Also it works as an attractor fly, and drawn fast across the surface at dusk it catches even more fish. Perhaps the trout think it is a Sedge.

The Dunkeld is another fly that has caught many rainbows and brown trout, as has the Butcher. The Jersey Herd worked fast or slow, deep or near the surface, is another winner, as is the Polystickle. Both of these are unashamedly small fish imitations, and are lures rather than flies. The Muddler Minnow is an American fly which in the yellow or 'Texas rose' shade is absolutely lethal. If I had to use one fly in a water containing rainbows, I would choose the Muddler!

Other flies I would not be without are Brown Nymphs, Green Nymphs, Pheasant-tail nymphs, Greenwells Glory, and Black Pennells. These last five flies are all winners in rivers too, for wet-fly fishing, and will keep you out of trouble on stony-bottomed lakes such as abound in Scotland. Scots trout are accustomed to looking up, down and every other way on account of there being less to eat in such places! Lake flies, incidentally, are usually a size or two larger than river flies, and the bigger lures are rather expensive. Stick to the list I've suggested, at least to start with. You will save money and catch plenty of trout.

7 Sea Angling Baits

Alan Wrangles

Although every year a number of newsworthy fish are caught on what might fairly be described as 'exotic' baits, by far the most consistent results are achieved by those who match their bait and technique to a more natural regime.

For example, the remains of a breakfast-time kipper might occasionally lure a large bass, but peeler or soft-back crab, sand eel or king ragworm are not only 'natural' baits, but they will also catch a greater number of a wider variety of fish with far greater regularity than scraps from the table.

However, this does not mean that you should stick rigidly to whatever is always used locally. Such a hidebound approach to angling can lead to a succession of blank days, and frequent excuses such as 'the wind is wrong', 'it's a bad tide', 'the fish are here, but they're not feeding'.

Most fish during the course of a year move around quite considerably. Their winter might be spent 160 km (100 miles) or more from where they are in the spring, and summer could see them even further from their winter quarters. Whilst travelling they will inevitably eat a wide variety of food, from other fish to worms, as well as perhaps mussels, whelks and cuttlefish.

Therefore, and whilst always respecting the time-honoured theory regarding 'fishing with local baits', I feel that on many occasions chances are missed because the subject of bait has not been fully considered.

As far as possible, try to take advantage of all that nature offers, not just what happens to be the local favourite.

For example, many years ago I accepted an invitation to fish with several friends in an estuary I had never previously visited, and therefore I was not certain about bait. However, I did know that lugworm could be dug within a few miles of where we were to fish, and so even if lugworm were not actually a part of the food supply in the estuary I felt that the fish were likely to be used to feeding on them.

I took a good supply of lugworm, only to be told on arrival that nobody ever used them locally, and in any case they were too soft for the style of fishing planned for the day. We were, I was told, going to be drifting around and expected to catch flounders or bass. We did just that, and using king ragworm, our bag of fish was respectable.

Eventually, I persuaded my two companions to anchor, change the style of fishing and use the lugworm which I didn't want to waste.

We turned to float tackle, and adjusted the stop on the line so that the bait was just tripping along the seabed. The result was not overwhelming, but it was comparable with what we had already achieved, and it proved to everyone's satisfaction that lugworm would catch fish, although the method had to suit both the conditions and the bait.

On subsequent trips to this estuary, and as a result of trying a variety of baits and methods at different times throughout the year, we all achieved results which surprised us.

One night whilst fishing with peeler and soft crab, we all caught a thornback ray or two, a fact which made many who regularly fished at night, but with ragworm, change their ways.

Quite recently I once again proved to my own satisfaction that not only the type of bait, but also its method of presentation can make all the difference between a good bag and a blank day.

Whilst boat fishing off the north-east coast of Ireland my companion and I used identical bait, rods, line and hook sizes; the only difference was a spoon lure. We fished an off-shore bank for flat fish, dabs mainly, and whilst my companion caught fish after fish on his spoon rig, the best I could do was attract the very occasional half-hearted 'nibble', but never a fish.

I changed bait, hook size, tried a longer and then shorter trace, and then various other rigs, all to no avail.

Not even the addition of a piece of white cuttle flesh would work, but on changing to a rig with a 3-cm (1½-in) chrome spoon some 12 to 15 cm (4 to 6 in) up from the hook, the fish started to come. We experimented for more than twelve hours, and throughout the period both lug and ragworm were accepted by the fish, but only when a spoon lure was part of the tackle.

There is far more to sea angling than just pushing a near-dead worm, or a piece of stale fish, on to a hook and then casting and waiting. Those who operate in this way are likely to catch fish more by accident than design.

At this juncture it is pertinent to remark on the importance of matching bait and hook. Whilst it is true that the unexpected in the form of a large tope or conger eel may come along and sweep up a bait being fished on tackle suited to flounder, it is still a fact that most anglers set out with the intention of catching a particular species of fish.

For example, when angling for tope it is quite possible that a ray or conger will take the bait, but that doesn't alter the fact that tope were being hunted. Similarly, the angler fishing for plaice or dabs might well end up by catching a flounder or a bass. But once again the basic intention, because of the situation, angling style and bait, was to catch the angler's original choice, namely a plaice.

In that one phrase, 'situation, angling style and bait' you have the essence of what is required to make a fishing trip successful; that is of course, if you add that other valuable ingredient, 'luck'. However, although there is always an element of luck in the success of any sportsman, never rely too heavily on it, for as a world-famous golfer once remarked to an admirer who mentioned luck, 'Yes, it is amazing, the more I practise the luckier I become'.

But to return to 'situation, style and bait' – within the term style I include the choice of hook, for the matching of bait and hook is a most important factor.

A thin wire hook with a long shank is ideal with a worm bait, and particularly so when fishing for species such as flounder and plaice. Not only will the worm be less damaged by such a hook, but a long shank can be removed more easily from within the relatively small mouth of a sole or dab.

In a later chapter the type of hook and bait suited to various species is considered in greater detail. Here I want to make the point that although collecting and using the right bait is important, all your efforts in this direction will be void if you fail to consider its relationship with the hook.

And so to collecting and storage. The former, if done incorrectly, can help to destroy the seashore environment, and the latter can rapidly turn fresh bait into an unusable mess. First, collection; and to do this efficiently you must know where to go, and how to set about the task of taking, but not spoiling, what you touch. Basically, the seashore is a natural larder, but like the larder in your home, if you leave the door open the flies or mice will come in and ruin the food.

Worms are extensively used by sea anglers. There are two main types, lug and ragworm, and they can be found in the zone between high- and low-water marks.

Lugworm inhabits sand, mud, or a mixture of the two. They betray their presence by throwing up a whirl on to the surface of the sand or mud – this cast is the remains of the material which the worm has passed through its body as it feeds.

Dig for them with a flat-pronged fork, and either turn over a selected area, digging as you would in your garden, or excavate single worms by selecting individual casts. Never dig holes and leave the foreshore pitted with bomb-like craters, few actions create more damage to the worm beds.

Whilst digging lugworm you may well find a few white

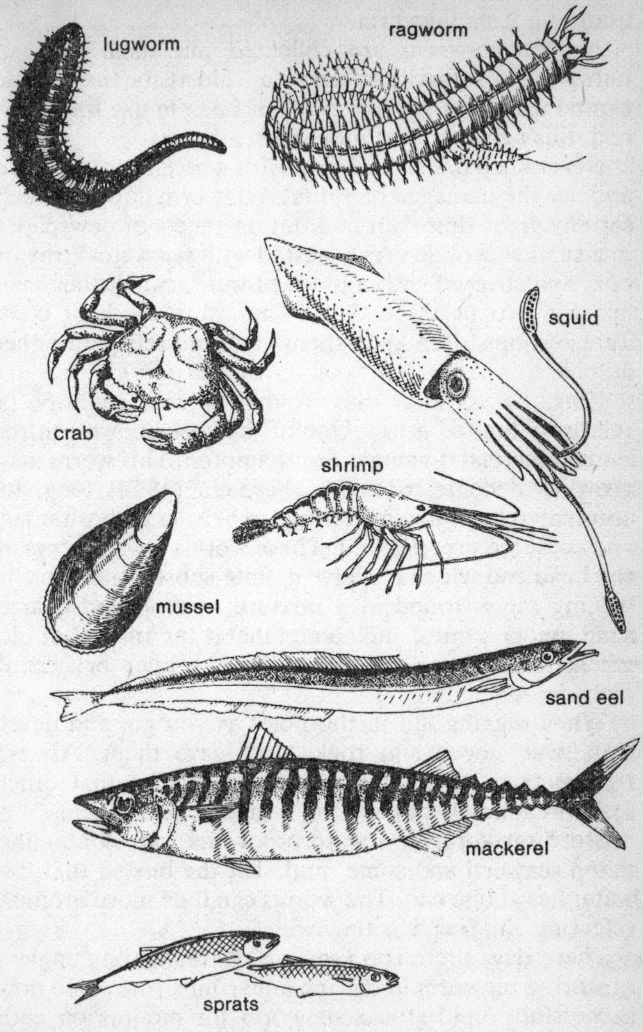

Various sea-fishing baits (not to scale)

ragworm. These are an excellent bait, but always separate rag from lugworm.

As the lugworm are collected put them into an untreated wooden box, never an old rusty tin. Plastic can be used, but my oak tray has been in use for years, and it has always been more than adequate.

Never keep damaged worm with whole ones, separate and use the damaged ones first. Lugworm does not keep for any great time, but laid out on sheets of newspaper in a shallow wooden (pre-wetted with sea water) tray or box, and covered with a piece of wet sacking, they may last for two or three days. They must be kept cool. Tackle shops often keep them in an old refrigerator set at 'cool'.

King ragworm is only found in any quantity in relatively limited areas. One of the best-known centres for commercial digging is Southampton. This worm may grow to become as much as 45 cm (18 in) long, its segmented body having a fringe of bristles on both sides, and coloured green to red. These worms have pincers at the head end which can give a quite substantial 'nip'.

King rag is found in a mixture of mud and coarse sand, under stones, and some inhabit the tip end of old whelk shells, even cohabiting with soldier or hermit crabs.

When digging, fill in the holes as you go, and never turn over stones and rocks and leave them. Always restore them to their original position, so that other seashore animals can use the refuge beneath them.

Store ragworm in a waterproof box, one containing damp seaweed and some mud. Tilt the box so that the water lies at one end. The worms can then move around, selecting either end as they will.

These days there is a growing custom among anglers of storing ragworm in marine aquariums, and some now successfully hold stocks of worm for months on end. However this is a skilled pastime, akin to keeping fish.

King rag supplied by tackle shops, which has travelled some distance, perhaps by rail, is often packed in vermiculite, a granulated plastic material. Although efficient, this does tend to 'dry' the worm after a day or so, and especially during warm weather.

Small red harbour ragworm is difficult to use, but it can be a deadly mullet bait.

Green shore crabs which scurry around the shore line make excellent bait at the time they are soft or peeling. In order to grow, a crab must change its shell, which it does at fairly regular intervals. When it is ready to 'moult' it goes into hiding under rocks, amid thick clumps of weed, or literally anywhere it stands a chance of being undisturbed whilst it is in its most vulnerable stage.

The hard shell on a 'peeler' is dull and listless, and can be lifted with your thumbnail. Left to its own devices, the crab will work itself out of its old shell, leaving the new soft covering to gradually harden. At either stage, as a 'peeler' or a 'soft back', crabs are excellent bait. As you collect them, drop them into an old haversack or sacking bag which has been half-filled with weed. Never mix soft and peeler crabs, they are cannibals, those with the hard shells, although they are losing them, will try to eat those with a soft shell.

If you have the facilities to store them, they will keep for some days in a suitably ventilated wooden bait box but they do need to be kept damp with sea water. They also need an amount of seaweed in with them. If possible, either collect them the day prior to fishing or go down when the tide is almost full out, find your bait and then fish.

Various species of fish make good baits, but these days, with prices being what they are, a whole new set of considerations apply. For example, herring is an exceptionally good bait, but it is difficult to justify using what is now an expensive and relatively scarce fish as bait to catch another species which may not be as good. Similarly, it is difficult to justify using mackerel, although currently they are still, in many areas, reasonably plentiful at certain times of the year. Therefore, seeing as mackerel can be caught without using another 'bait' (they are taken on lures such as feather-dressed hooks), these are for me the most important of all fish baits.

Sprats can also be used, as can pout, smelt and other small species. Sand eel, an excellent fish bait, is seldom available live, though in frozen form they can be successful, but less so, in my opinion.

Molluscs – and from the angler's standpoint this means cuttle and squid – are both long-lasting, easily handled, effective and are capable of being employed in a variety of ways.

When boat fishing, cuttle may be picked up at sea, but always take care as, like octopus, their body contains an ink-sac which holds a fluid capable of creating an indescribable mess. Pick the body up in a net and drop it into a bucket and cut the flesh away from the bone. If the ink-sac breaks, wash the flesh immediately, and dump the remains overboard. Cuttle tentacles, strips of flesh or the whole head all make excellent baits, and the flesh can be frozen to use another day.

Squid, usually available from tackle shops and some fishmongers, is normally sold in a frozen state. As bait it is similar to cuttle.

Shellfish, in my opinion, fall into two categories; those which are good baits but difficult to use, and those which are easy to use, but make poor baits. Mussel is a good example of the former; and cockles, no more than a fair standby bait, fall into the latter category.

For a variety of reasons, pollution being one of them, mussels are no longer as plentiful as they used to be. However, for boat fishing (or where casting isn't important) they are a good bait. You just push a knife-tip into the broad end, and without separating the two shells, run the knife blade around the line. Once the muscle inside the shell at the broad end is severed, the shell will open quite easily. You can then push the hook tip into the brown/purple 'foot' and wrap the remainder of the flesh around the hook. Finally you can push the hook tip through a section of the cut muscle.

It is also possible to hold the mussel in place by putting a section of worm tail, or a small piece of fish, on to the hook point.

Slipper limpet is another good bait, particularly after a storm, where areas of beach become littered with them. Fish come in close to feed on them as the making tide washes them back. They can be left for a day or two to become 'high' – some anglers say they are much better bait in that condition. Just take the flesh out of the shell.

Razor fish, clams, piddocks, etc., will all catch fish, but frequently these shellfish are now so difficult to find it is not worth wasting time looking for them. But they can be used as bait – if and when you have the opportunity to collect them.

Cockles are sometimes part of a professional fishery – so ask before collecting them.

Both prawn and shrimps can be killing baits, but, and this is only repeating what I have already written, if you find a supply of prawn or shrimps, can you really justify using them as bait? I think I would rather cook and eat them!

Bread, in its various bait forms, e.g. flake, crust, cubes, etc., is often an excellent bait for mullet. Some mix bread into a paste with the oil from a can of sardines and undoubtedly it can work, but personally I have never found it to be any more effective than a piece of flake.

There are many other items, both animal and vegetable, that have at one time or another caught fish. Indeed, as Brian Watts wrote at the beginning of the chapter dealing with freshwater baits, 'Almost anything the angler can eat, plus many items that he can't can be used . . .' but despite some omissions, I am sure that the foregoing will provide a list of baits that will lure almost any fish you are likely to encounter around the British Isles.

8 *Anglers' Knots*

Ken Whitehead

Ask any fisherman who has just lost a large fish how it happened, and he will usually blame his rod, reel, line or hook, in fact anything but the probable cause, namely the failure of one of the several knots he tied whilst assembling the tackle.

In this chapter we are primarily concerned with nylon monofilament, a special material which requires specialised knots, although braided line as well as nylon-covered steel wire, is used by sea anglers.

It is important to realise that when tying a knot in line which has been made by twisting slivers and strands together, like string, by crossing the line in a certain way, one twist grips against another and so helps to create a knot which will not slip when under strain.

When nylon monofilament, or single-strand line, was developed, it soon became obvious that a whole new range of knots was needed, as the traditional ones just didn't work properly. It is also vital to understand that when a knot is tied in nylon mono it reduces the overall strength of the line by a substantial amount, in some cases by as much as 30 per cent, even when a correct knot has been well tied. A knot which has been hastily tied and over-stretched as it is pulled together can result in the loss of as much as 50 per cent of the line's original strength.

Now this might not be too drastic if you were fishing with 45-kg (100-lb) B.S. line, for in theory, the 22·6-kg (50-lb) strength you have left should be sufficient to allow you to beat a fish weighing 68 kg (150 lb) or more. But this doesn't necessarily happen in practice. Other factors such as shock loading, possible damage to the line caused by abrasion as it chafes against rocks and stones, and even the fish itself, can all mean the line is subjected to a greater strain than theory suggests.

Consider fishing with a 0·9- or 1·3-kg (2- or 3-lb) B.S. line – what is your safety margin then? Every time that a hook, a swivel, or a lead is fastened there can be a drastic loss of line power, all of which only add up to lost fish.

No single knot is capable of securing every item of tackle to the line, nor of coping with all the strains and stresses that occur while fishing. As I mentioned at the beginning of the chapter, there are firstly the differences between braided and monofilament line to contend with. Then knots often have to be tied in various places on a line, and may need to pass through a hole or perhaps over a lip, or, for instance, through the end ring on a rod. If the knot is very big, it may jam and prevent movement. Therefore, small streamlined knots are needed for these situations, and if you study the blood knot you will understand why it is used for fly lines and casts.

To be successful, the all-round angler needs to know how to tie at least six knots, to be capable of tying them in the dark, with freezing cold fingers, or in any sort of material, and to know where and when to use them. Each of the essential knots is shown here in step-by-step pictures, and their various uses are listed. Study them all carefully, and then practise each using a smooth piece of string or a thick piece of monofilament before trying to produce an expert knot when actually fishing.

Half-blood knot

This is used for fastening swivels, leads or hooks to the line, or for tying on any item that has a solid eye through which the line must be passed.

Start by passing the line through the eye, and twisting it six times. Then pass the end of the line through the loop next to the eye. Now pass the end through the loop at the back of the twist, and pull it gently together. Cut off the end.

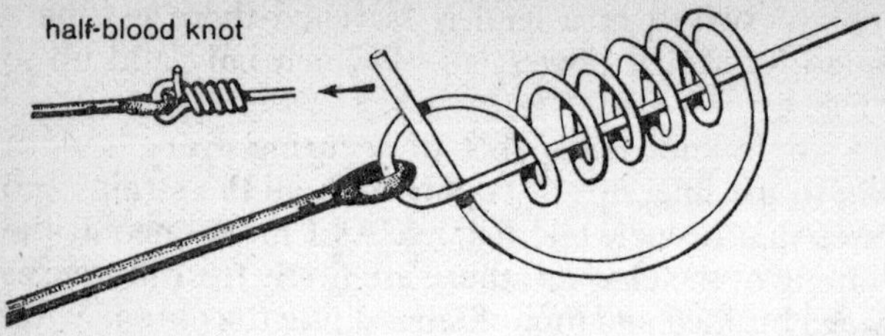
half-blood knot

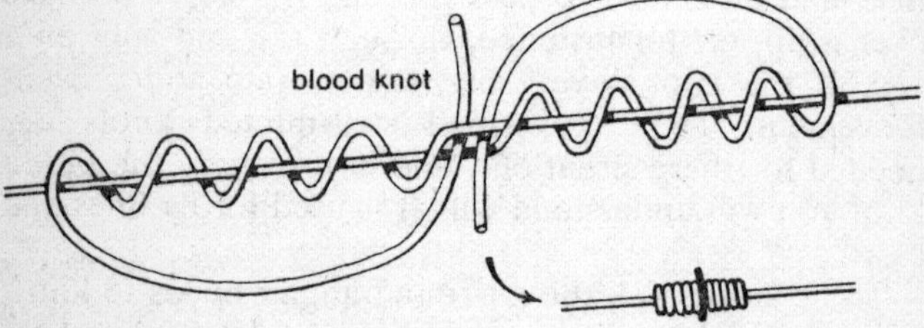
blood knot

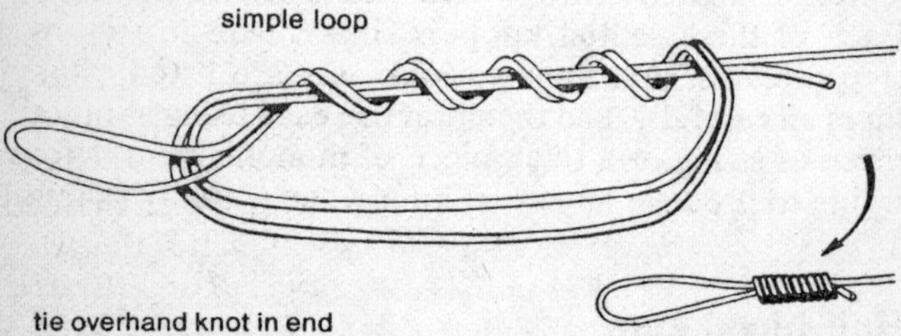
simple loop

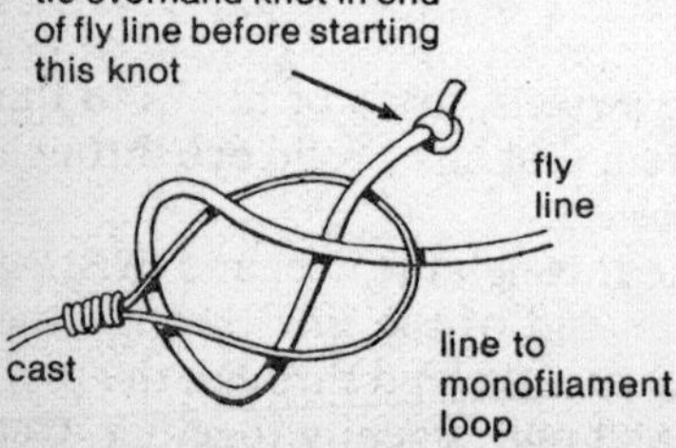
tie overhand knot in end of fly line before starting this knot
fly line
cast
line to monofilament loop

Blood knot

This is an essential knot where two lengths of monofilament are to be joined together, even if they are of unequal diameter, and where the knot must pass through a ring.

Start by crossing the ends of the line over each other, then twist one end around the body of the other line four or five times before tucking it back between the two parts at the start of the twist. Now repeat the process with the other end, twisting in the opposite direction. Finish by passing that end through the centre loop. Gently ease the knot together and pull firm before cutting off the loose ends.

Simple loop

Whenever you need a loop in the end of the line, this is the knot to use. Double the end back on itself and then form a loop. Twist the loop four or five times and then pass the tip of the doubled line through the twisted loop. Pull it up tight, cutting off the end.

Line to monofilament loop

Where you need to fasten a heavy line (fly or braided nylon) to a monofilament cast, this is the knot to use.

Form a simple loop in the monofilament and then tie an overhand knot in the end of the heavy line. Now pass the knotted line through the loop, pass it behind the loop and tuck it under itself inside the cast loop. Pull firmly together.

Turle knot

An easy knot for fastening a cast to a fly. Pass the line through the eye of the hook and then tie an ordinary turle knot — the loop is passed over the hook

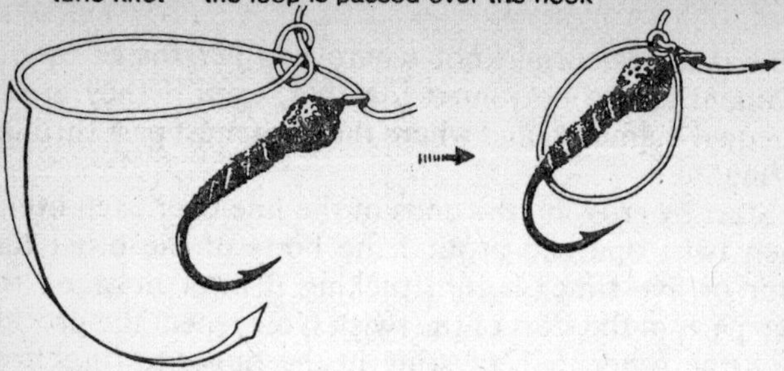

dipped loops

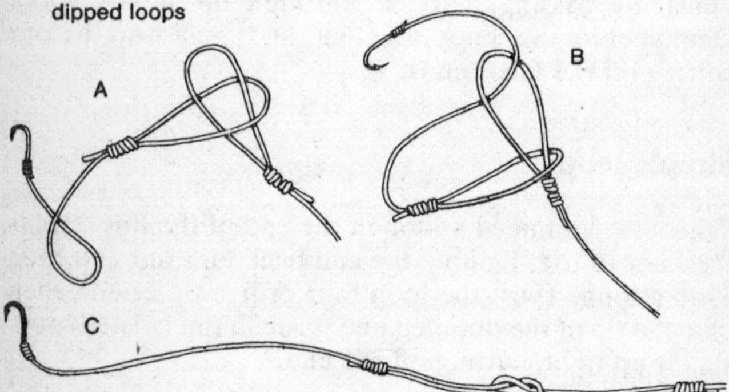

shock leader

shock leader knot — for tying a leader of heavy nylon to main line

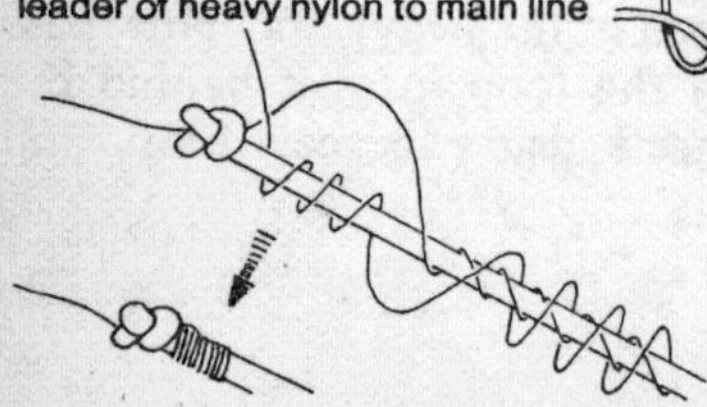

blood loop dropper knot — for tying nylon paternoster

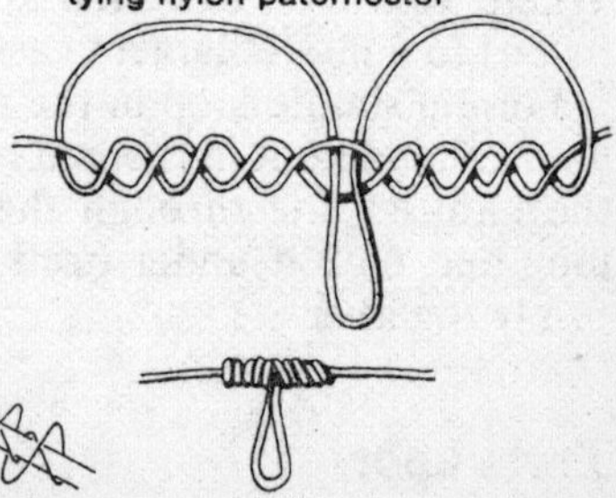

Shock leader and dropper knots are used in sea fishing

overhand knot in its end. Pass the loop over the hook and tighten it around the shank of the hook below the eye. Tighten it and cut the end free.

Dipped loops

Very small match fishing hooks are tied to a short length of nylon with a loop at the opposite end. An easy way of fastening this length is to tie a simple loop in the reel line, then hold a loop in each hand and pass the right-hand loop through the left-hand one. Pass the end that is free from the left-hand loop through the right-hand loop and pull until the loops are interlocked.

When there is a loose end to be cut free use a pair of sharp scissors if possible. A blunt or heavy cut from a knife will bruise and damage the short length of line that is left, and this often leads to knot failure. Don't use a flame to burn off the end, as heat weakens synthetic lines. Where the line has to be pulled together to form the knot, pull it gently, and moisten the knot with a little saliva to help ease it in place.

Finally, look carefully at each knot when you have finished tying it. If you are not satisfied with it, cut it free and start again. If you don't, you can be sure that one day *you* will be telling a story about 'the one that got away'.

9 Coarse Fishing Methods: River

Brian Watts

The object of coarse fishing is, naturally, to catch fish, therefore the angler must first know where to look for them, and nowhere is this more true than on the wild and turbulent rivers in the North-east. However, no matter where you fish, it is true to say that fish are not to be found in every part of the river, but gather in shoals where the water is right for them. They like certain places, and these can change with the seasons or conditions.

Applied logic helps, and so 'think fish' is a key phrase. The angler who can envisage what is happening below the river surface, and why, is most likely to succeed. On still waters it is relatively easy, the fish are either well out or sheltering under banksides. If the wind is warmer than the water they will be near the bank it is blowing towards, and if the wind is colder, the fish move to the sheltered side.

On rivers, identifying where the fish are likely to be is more difficult, but far more interesting. Study the flow of the water which brings them food, and also look for overhanging vegetation from which insects drop. Read the water; a turbulence or swirl on the surface will betray an underwater obstruction. Even check the material of the river bed – is it mud, sand, gravel or rock? Fish seldom stay over slab rock in cold weather, but a place where the flow cuts into and under the bankside provides a nice holding spot for them.

Try throwing a few floating chrysalises on to the water, and watch as the current takes them away. Downriver fish may rise to take them and a shoal is located!

Before actually committing yourself to fishing a swim,

make sure it is clear of obstructions. There is no point in preparing your swim with groundbait only to find it too snaggy to fish. So the fish are less likely to see you, set up your tackle back from the bank edge and off the skyline and wear clothing which blends with the background – greens and browns, not reds and blues. If wading, make use of any shadows caused by trees, and when bank fishing, watch for a handy bush which may give some cover.

Also, give careful thought to your tackle. For example a float must be chosen with three things in mind: the maximum distance to which you will have to cast and the depth and flow of water. You may select a 5 BB size, so shot up to suit, bearing in mind the more shot you place high up towards the float, the slower the bait will sink, and as a general rule do not place shot nearer than 30 cm (12 in) to the hook. On most occasions, a size 16 hook is ideal when float fishing and using a double maggot bait. Nick the maggot on to the hook through the point at its 'blunt' end.

After adding water to mix the groundbait, leave it to absorb and set for about ten minutes. Used too quickly it may float uselessly down river on the surface. Maggots mixed with the groundbait are a useful way of getting samples of hook bait down quickly at the head of a swim in fast-flowing water.

If maggots are your bait, make sure they are clean of sawdust, for this will taint the groundbait and might also blow into your eyes when throwing them into the swim.

Check that the swim is free of snags by casting to the head of it and allowing the tackle to travel right down, adjusting the float depth until the bait just trips bottom.

If the swim is clear, now get the fish interested. You may be on a gravel run, the type favoured by dace. Ensure the float is as low in the water as possible, but still visible – the lower it sits the easier the fish can pull it under, and the longer they will hold on. This creates a valuable time lag, and enables you to strike and set the hook.

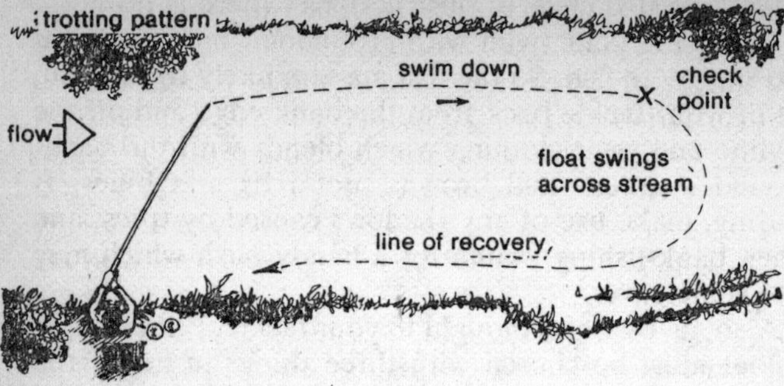
trotting pattern
swim down
check point
flow
float swings across stream
line of recovery

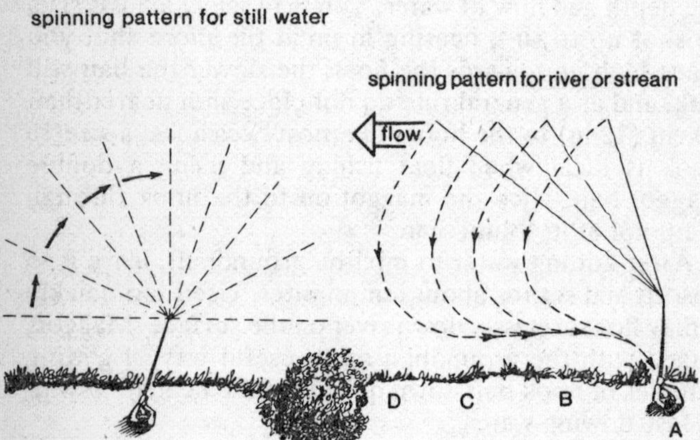
spinning pattern for still water
spinning pattern for river or stream
flow
D
C
B
A

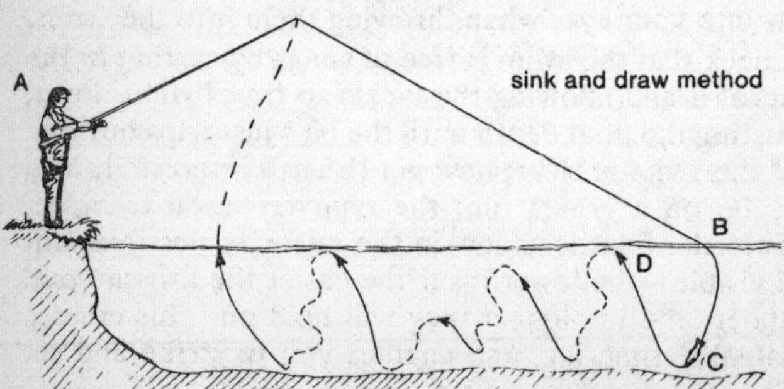
sink and draw method
A
B
D
C

The pattern you choose to feed the swim is very important. Loose feed, in this case maggots, must be introduced at the head of the swim, not too many, just a small handful. They will drift downstream, sinking slowly, and fish will move into the swim in line with this food supply. Keep adding another handful of maggots every second cast, and keep it up, even when fish are coming regularly. This is vital. However, do not use groundbait in water so clear that you can see the bottom, nor, as a general rule, in shallow swims. Fish will seldom feed in such circumstances for they are then exposed to too much danger from their predators.

Fish will soon respond to action of this sort, so be prepared to increase or decrease the number of maggots. If you are overfeeding, the fish will drop downstream chasing maggots which pass them, and you will have to trot your float further downstream for each succeeding bite. Usually a bite is quite positive. The float tip vanishes, and only a slight flick of the rod will set the hook.

As the rod bucks to the pull of the fish – and even quite small dace pull well in the full run of the stream – apply side strain and move the fish out of the shoal. A gentle but firm pressure should suffice. Dace are a shoal fish, and the 'fear' signal from a hooked fish will panic the rest, so it must be eased out quickly.

In some rivers, particularly some of those in the North, swims are short, really little more than pools between rapids or shallows. Chub often take up a position at the bottom end of such pools, just where the bottom starts to run up. They take fright easily, so do not try and get too close. Let the streams do the work, carrying the float down to them, and be ready for the quick lunge as a chub strikes at the bait. Once hooked, apply upward pressure and get the fish's head and mouth out of the water. Once you achieve this all fight dies,

Middle, opposite: *points A, B, C and D are each 2 or 3 paces apart;* Below: *bait is cast from A to B, allowed to sink and lie for a minute at C then drawn up to D and the pattern repeated.*

and the fish can be slid smoothly over the landing net. Be warned, if you let the chub dip under again, it will immediately respond with a strong lunge, and will sometimes break free.

During the summer when there is heavy weed growth, look for the narrow streams of clear water separating the weed banks. Fish find both shelter and food amongst the plant life, and your task is to tempt them out. Introduce maggot feed as before, and trot your float tackle down as near to the weed as possible. You will probably need to wade to get into position to do this with reasonable control. Clear all the interested fish from a weed bed and when the bites stop, move down to the next one. You will need your keepnet fastened to you for this type of fishing. A short bankstick thrust through your belt or down a wader leg may suffice, although anglers who frequently fish this way often have special belts and 'screw-on plates' made by a local craftsman. Such adaptations are not sold in tackle shops.

Grayling is another species likely to be found over gravel runs, but its determination to keep to clean water has forced the fish into the upper reaches of some rivers such as the Yare, Swale and Tees, and it is not found in the Wear or Tyne. Grayling are strong fighters with a large dorsal fin and a 'twisting' feel when hooked. They give off a strong smell of cucumber when landed and they feed best in cold winter weather.

Grayling have a soft mouth, and shed a hook very easily. Use a small hook, size 18 or 20, with a lighter than usual trace length for these fish. Maggot is an acceptable bait, but a brandling worm or sweetcorn often tempts better quality fish, especially when backed up with some loose maggot fed as groundbait.

Barbel are native to a relatively small number of rivers. These bottom-feeding fish lie in faster water, favouring gravel beds at the tail end of rapids or where the river flows strongly on the outside of bends. They are taken on float tackle, but often this happens when the angler is really fishing for another species – possibly chub. Usually, leger tackle is more appropriate for barbel fishing, and sometimes a rolling leger is more effective than one which is static.

Split shot can be moved individually or collectively to wherever on the line, between float and hook, they bring the best response from the fish. Moving shot up the line – even to immediately below the float – will mean the bait will sink more slowly and more naturally. And this also works in reverse. If the fish are feeding really well on the river bottom, move the shot down, even to 30 cm (12 in) above the hook, so the bait gets down quickly to where the fish are. It speeds up the catch rate.

Changing the depth at which you are fishing can have a marked effect on the way the tackle moves downstream. By moving the float closer to the hook, the bait will be lifted off the bottom and travelling at stream speed. Try letting it go smoothly with no check on the line. If this does not work, try edging the bait through the swim, feeding line off the spool at a slower rate than the flow of the water.

Under these conditions, by all means try nearer and mid-stream swims first, but if bites do not come be prepared to fish the far bank, even if there is deep water in mid-river, and under the far bank it is shallow. Wading is sometimes necessary under these conditions but never enter the water unless you must, and be very careful, never wade through deep water.

Lying on

When rivers are in flood, or during cold winter months, different tactics are often called for. Frequently, swims to be found virtually under your feet will hold fish under these conditions, and the 'lying on' style will often bring success when all other methods fail. A spot where tree roots or bankside debris overhang deep water offers cover to fish. Here, an Avon or similar deep-bodied float capable of taking enough shot to keep the bait hard on

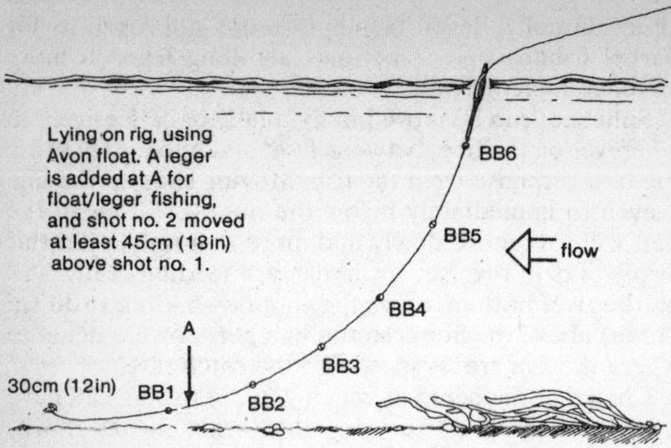

Lying on rig, using Avon float. A leger is added at A for float/leger fishing, and shot no. 2 moved at least 45cm (18in) above shot no. 1.

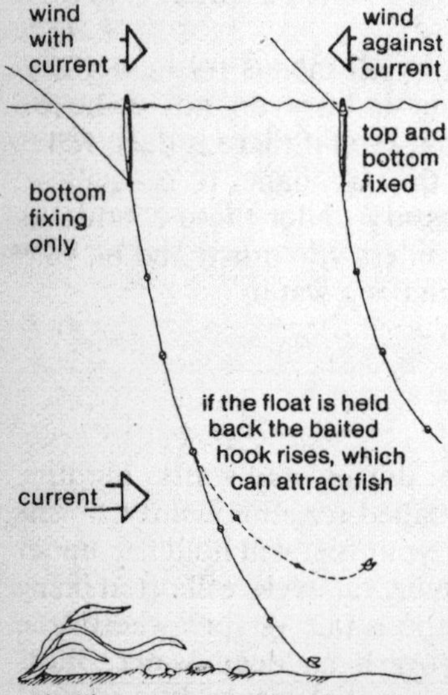

trotting a stream with and against the wind

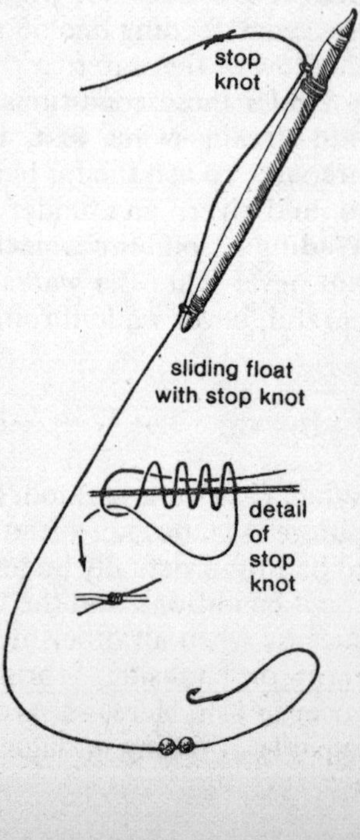

sliding float with stop knot

the bottom of the river should be used. Extra split shot will be needed to overcome the increased buoyancy of the float and most of the shot will be placed down near the hook.

Casting and striking

Use a plummet to establish the depth at the point you are fishing and set the float to give at least 60 cm (2 ft) more line than the depth of water.

Do not just drop the tackle in, cast well out into the river and then reel back slowly. This will lie the baited hook neatly along the river bed and it will swing in to rest against the debris or roots without much danger of becoming snagged.

Keep the rod tip low, tighten the line between rod and float and feed groundbait into the swim so it carpets the river bed around the hook. Usually a slight movement warns that a bite is imminent, and a positive take will dip the float under. As you strike and the hook goes home, expect the fish to move out into the flow in an attempt to escape. So be ready to apply gentle but firm pressure on the line to prevent him from doing so.

On other occasions it might pay to move the float up the line so that the bait is being fished 'over-depth'. For best results shot should be actually resting on the river bed. Again, you can trot through the swim with the line flowing freely off the spool, or retard the play-off, when the effects will be completely different. Running freely, the float goes ahead of the tackle with the bottom shot acting as a drag-anchor, slowing down the bait. The strike has to be rather harder than with other methods, for there is more loose line to pick up. Holding back whilst fishing over-depth needs practice, but it can account for many fish. Ease the float through the swim and remember what is happening underwater. The bait is ahead of the float, and depending on how hard you hold back the line, it will have lifted to some degree off the river bed. The bite will be fast, but with no loose line to recover the fish is still easy to hook.

When fish come off the hook as you strike, you get what some anglers describe as a 'bounce' feeling. You should check the hook. It may have lost its point against a rock, and so have failed to penetrate the fish's jaw.

On the River Swale, one of the best coarse anglers in the area has a formula for fishing. 'Just walk along the bank until you see the fish,' he says, 'then catch them.' He likes to wade into the top end of a pool, and staying close to the bank edge carefully downstream, the fish moving away from him until they are 'pinned' at the end of the pool. Next, by fishing carefully and quietly, he takes a good many of these fish before they panic. Obviously this technique is only possible on certain rivers.

A mainly shallow river produces fish which are wary and keen-eyed, so they usually spot the angler very quickly and they will move over to lie under the opposite bank. Where trees have fallen and are lying close in against the bank, or where there is a mass of tree roots in the water, the 'lying on' method can be used to search for fish under the debris. Just keep increasing the distance between float and hook, and remember the guiding principle: cast out and then reel in so the bait swings under the debris.

Float legering

Some deeper swims may be better suited to the 'float leger' system. Where a bankside swim offers only a narrow band of free water between two trees or bushes, or where there is fast-flowing deep water near the bank the bait is presented stationary, hard on the bottom. While this method does not allow you to search under vegetation, it is ideal for 'stepping' along the river bed in stages. Hold the float back hard, and then release and lift to move the leger to a new position.

‘Counting method’

There are certain stretches on various rivers where the water is deep, possibly close to the bank, where fish might be lying at virtually any depth. Here, a technique known to some as the ‘counting method’, or to others as ‘fishing on the drop’, can be most effective. First, it is important to encourage the fish to start feeding, and so distribute a supply of maggots into the swim steadily and regularly. Set the split shot so that the hook sinks slowly, beginning with as little as 1 metre (3 ft) between hook and float. Gradually increase the distance, and every cast count the seconds between the moment the bait hits the water and when the float cocks. When the float fails to cock at the very second it should, strike, for a fish will have taken the bait. You also will have located the depth at which they are feeding.

In winter, a true leger arrangement is as effective on many occasions as float tackle. Where roach, dace and chub shoal in large numbers in deeper, quicker swims, a swing or quiver tip is needed to provide quick bite detection and to hook a fast-biting fish. Remembering that dace are particularly quick, methods worth considering include a swim feeder linked on the line about 30 cm (1 ft) above the hook; feeding loose maggots past the hookbait will help to encourage fish to bite fast and a maggot feeder with an Arlesey bomb leger weight fitted into it is a particularly popular device.

Swing or quiver tip bites are usually quite positive, easily identifiable by a novice as a true ‘bite’ rather than movement on the tip created by a breeze. However, despite the undoubted efficiency of legering techniques, float fishing does, in my opinion, take fish more rapidly when they are feeding well. Therefore, I always have a float-fishing rod tackled and ready for use, just in case circumstances change and a quick switch would prove beneficial.

At one time, when centre-pin reels were widely used, swift recovery of a hooked fish was achieved by using a technique referred to as 'batting'. Once the fish was hooked, and here we are considering small species such as dace or roach of 170 g (6 oz) or so, the reel spool was struck rapidly by the palm of a hand (i.e. 'batted'), and this action spun the spool rapidly, picking up line as fast as possible, the fish being literally skimmed over the surface on its side. This is really a 'speed-fishing' technique, one which is often used by match anglers taking part in a competition. Under these circumstances speed is the basis of the whole operation, as tackle which is out of the water doesn't catch fish!

These days, because centre-pin reels are not much used, 'batting' is to a large extent a thing of the past, although 'speed fishing' is still important. Fixed spool reels can be used to 'skim fish', but it takes practice, and fish are often lost whilst acquiring the art. As you strike, a slight jerk pops the fish to the surface, then fast reeling action will keep it up and 'skim' it in. Lift the rod tip as the fish reaches a point about two rods' lengths away, and keep reeling and lifting. The fish will then swing into your hand – it just takes practice!

Eels, a species which you either hate or love, are best taken on leger tackle. One important factor in their favour is that eels from nice clean rivers make excellent eating, and in many countries are considered a great delicacy, particularly in Holland and Germany.

Eel bites are very positive, but a swing or spring tip is recommended when leger fishing for them, as the bite is seen that much sooner, and so may prevent the fish from gorging the bait. A lip-hooked eel is much easier to free. When unhooking them, hold these slime-covered creatures in a piece of wet cloth to avoid damaging them with your hands.

Take care!

And so to the most important of all the many aspects of angling, your personal safety.

I live in the North-east where flash floods and deep pools with rocky ledges which end abruptly are two major hazards. The River Swale can rise 3 metres (10 ft) in as many minutes following heavy rain in the Pennines, and you may not know it is falling because it may not be raining where you are. Even in good weather the river can come up with little or no warning.

Many an angler has had to be rescued from rocks and islands in the middle of flooded rivers. It is vital that every angler should get to know local danger signs, wherever he or she lives and fishes.

Never wade in a stream you don't know, or one where others never wade, and in any case never do so unless you have a companion present to lend a hand if necessary. Always fish from the bank where you can.

Never fish from a position in which you cannot land a big fish; remember that slab rock can be very slippery, and loss of balance can lead to tragedy.

Look out for banks which have been undercut by the current. When such a bank collapses, it can do so without warning, and dump you and your tackle into an icy cold river. Even if the water is only a foot or so deep, it can be very unpleasant.

Plants can also create problems; from stinging nettles to giant hogwort, there are many things to avoid.

Giant hogwort, a massive thick-stemmed umbrella-type vegetation, has become established in the River Tees area, and now grows prolifically on parts of the river bank to well over head height. The stems, if scraped, give off a sap which creates a painful rash or blisters on bare skin. This can last for several days and be very unpleasant.

If fishing alone, make sure someone at home knows where you are – in case something goes wrong.

Angling is a wonderful pastime, which takes you into beautiful surroundings. *Always* remember to leave the countryside as you found it, leaving not a scrap of litter nor bits of discarded tackle behind, and take care to come home safely.

10 Still Water Fishing

Ken Whitehead

Still water fishing poses many problems not faced by river anglers. For example, the quarry has time to inspect and reject a bait if it so desires, whereas the fish in running water has only a limited time to consider and decide whether or not food is acceptable before it is swept away by the current. Also, in some instances, the species are different. For example, neither carp nor tench would, as a general rule, be found inhabiting a streamy shallow run between banks of weed, whereas they would be found in still water.

So although the angler can still use tackle which is basically very similar to that used when fishing a stream, there will be a difference in the strength, arrangement and general style of angling, alterations which make all the difference between success and failure.

Carp – common, mirror and leather – are the real freshwater heavyweights, and fish of 13 kg (30 lb) or more are taken most seasons, as are a large number in the 4- to 9-kg (10- to 20-lb) weight bracket. Mirror and leather carp are similar to the common, except for skin and scales. They are mutations of the common species, and for all angling purposes can be dealt with in a similar manner.

Tench, which possess very small scales, and in fact appear practically scale-less, are an interesting species to fish for.

Crucian carp are a relatively small species, and a fish of 0·9 kg (2 lb) or so can be considered quite a catch.

When considering tackle, it must be assumed that on occasions long casting will be needed, and so any rod the angler uses must be both strong and pliable. Rods suited to this type of angling are usually 3 to 3·3 m (10 to 11 ft) in length and have two sections. You must make sure that the rod is not so heavy that you cannot

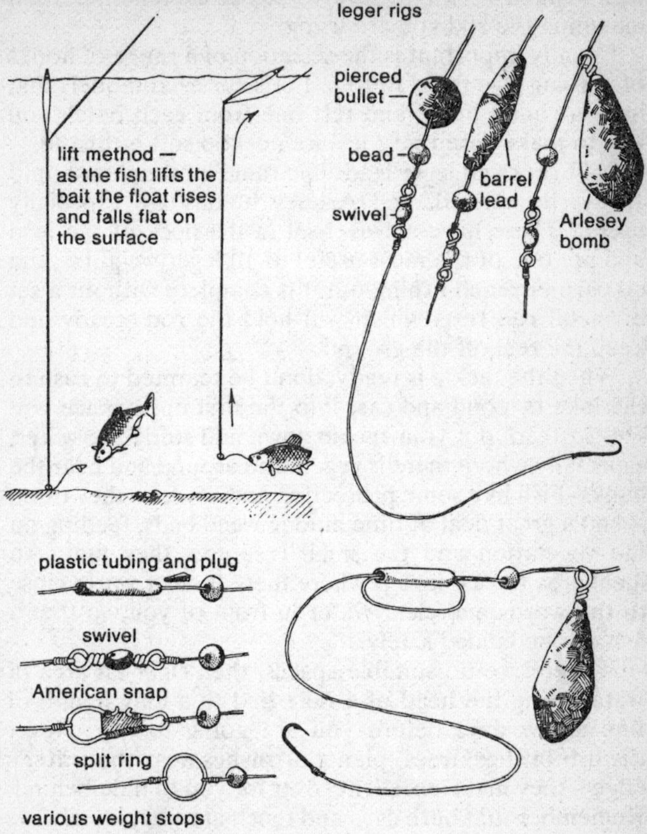

manage it properly, and also that the cork handle is comfortable to hold.

A medium-size fixed-spool reel will complement such a rod, and will allow easy casting with very positive line control. Buy the best you can afford, and choose one that has a drum designed to hold a decent length of line.

Good line is an expensive item, and it should be protected from excessive heat or sunlight, both of which will weaken it. Make sure to select a breaking strain matching the rod you are using.

Equally important is the selection of a range of hooks of varying size from 10 to 6. Look for eyed models that have a round bend, and test one from each batch you buy to make sure that they are not too soft or brittle.

Split shot and leger leads in a range of weights should always be carried, and Arlesey bombs are especially useful. These have a swivel set in the neck of the lead and are one of the most useful of all leger weights. And no carp or tench fishing outfit is complete without a set of metal rod rests which will hold the rod steady and keep the reel off the ground.

When the tackle is ready, don't be tempted to rush to the lake or pond and cast into the first open space you see. Instead, put your tackle down and study the water, especially where there is vegetation around and near the banks. Fish like some protection and cover so they often spend a great deal of time among weed beds, feeding on the vegetation and the small creatures they find. An ideal area to cast into is where there is clear water close to the weeds and clear water in front of you, so that a fish can be landed safely.

If there are no suitable spaces, then clear an area of water using the head of a rake tied to a long length of line a few days before you are going to fish. Never disturb bushes, trees, plants or rushes near the water's edge – they make excellent cover for you to hide behind. Remember that both carp and tench are wary, so always assemble your tackle well back from the water, and then move gently into position.

Carp and tench feed on the bottom, and there is a very useful and extremely sensitive way of fishing for them called a one-shot rig.

Fasten a float by the bottom end to the line either with a float cap or by taking two or three turns through the float ring, but do not fasten the top of the float in any way. Attach the hook to the line, and about 10 cm (4 in) above the hook place one large-sized (BB) shot on to the line.

Check the water's depth and slide the float up the line until the distance between it and the shot equals the depth of water in front of you; then bait up and cast out. The float should settle with its bottom end just dipped below the surface. Lay groundbait around the float and settle down to wait, taking care to keep below the skyline and away from the water's edge. Once a fish takes the bait and lifts it from the bottom, the shot will also be lifted and so the float will lie completely flat. As the fish moves with the bait the float will slide under the surface, and that will be the moment to make the strike.

Fishing without a float – legering – is yet another method of presenting a bait on the bottom, and it is a method which is usually practised where the bait has to be placed a long way from the bank, or when the water is rough.

Start by sliding an Arlesey bomb on to the main line, then add a leger stop, a plastic device to prevent the lead sliding down the line to the hook. The stop should be fastened 45 cm (18 in) above the hook. Bait up and cast, taking care not to jerk the rod and so lose the bait. Once the lead has sunk, settle the rod into the rests, recover any loose line and set a bite indicator. This can be a folded piece of metal baking foil clipped over the line between the bail arm and the first rod ring. As a fish moves off with the bait the foil will move, showing it is time to make the strike.

If there is thick mud on the lake or pond bed, then the chances are that a heavy weight will sink down, taking the bait with it. To overcome these conditions fold a strong piece of monofilament over the reel line, securing it with several split shot. These weights can be stopped from reaching the hook by pinching a large split shot on to the line. The line will slide freely, and is unlikely to sink far into the mud. It is a very sensitive arrangement.

Carp are very fond of taking food from the surface of

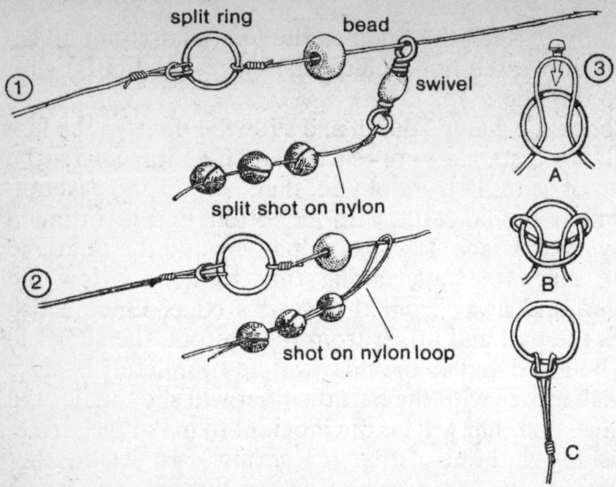

Link legers: 1 with swivel; 2 with nylon loop. 3 Split ring is attached to main line by passing the loop up through the ring (A), and taking the top of the loop over the ring (B). (C) shows the completed knot.

the water, and there is an excellent chance of catching them when they do so by using a floating bait. This is a particularly good method during the warm months of the year. No weight is required for this style of fishing, just a large hook, size 6 or thereabouts, and a large crust of bread cut or pulled from a loaf. This bait is mounted on the hook dunked into the water to give it some weight, then cast gently out on to the surface usually near to the bank or a bed of water lilies. Once it is settled in its place, stand the rod in the rests and watch for signs of interest. Usually a carp will suck at the bait for a time before it takes the whole piece in its mouth; do not get over-excited, wait to strike until the bread disappears completely.

Pike are also 'heavyweights', or at least, they can be. Individual fish weighing as much as 13 kg (30 lb) or slightly more are landed every season, and the biggest usually come from either still or very slow-moving water.

Generally speaking, the type of rod already mentioned as suited to carp fishing will do for pike, as will the reel and line. A large landing net is also essential, but the end tackle, those parts which fasten to the line, will be very different. Round pike floats with a hole drilled completely through the centre, a supply of small beads, some BB shot, small swivels and a selection of Jardine snap tackles should be chosen, with some help from your tackle dealer.

To set these together, first snip a length of nylon from the end of your line, and tie a stop knot on to the line itself. Below this place a small bead and then a float. Fix a snap tackle using a small swivel, between the line and trace, and clamp enough shot on to the line to cock the float. Fix the treble hooks into a large dead sprat or small herring and slide the stop knot up the line, so that the float, when it is held by the bead resting against the stop, allows the dead bait to lie on the bottom.

Although some still practise live baiting for pike, the technique cannot really be justified on any practical angling grounds. Dead baits such as sprat, etc., are easily available and they catch just as many fish.

Usually the float will make small movements before a pike starts a run, but making the right decision regarding the moment to strike can be difficult. Too soon and the bait will only just be in the pike's mouth and the hooks will pull free . . . too late and the pike will have swallowed the bait. A good general rule is to wait until the float has moved several feet away from the point at which it disappeared, and as you strike, wind in line between the float and the rod tip, pulling the rod back firmly and to one side of your body as you do so. Never snatch, and remember to keep the line tight all the time a fish is being played.

When you land a pike, or indeed any species of fish, never panic! Sink the landing net below the surface of the water in front of you, and hold it steady. Draw the fish over the net then lift the net up and on to the bank. Never jab at the fish with the net, and always move well back from the water's edge before you try to unhook the fish.

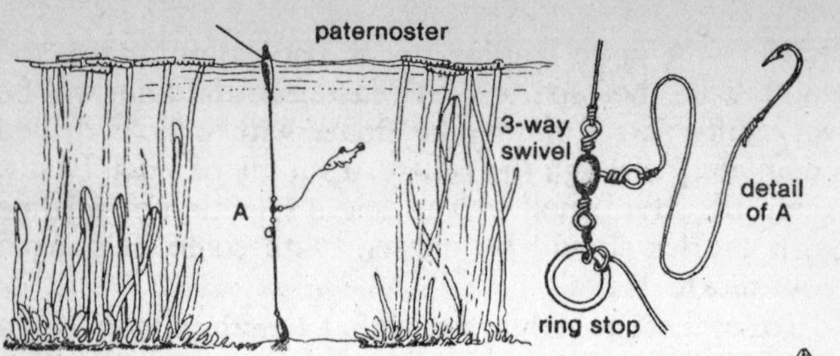

a dead sprat mounted for sink and draw style of fishing — the line is drawn through the body using a baiting needle; the hook is drawn into the vent

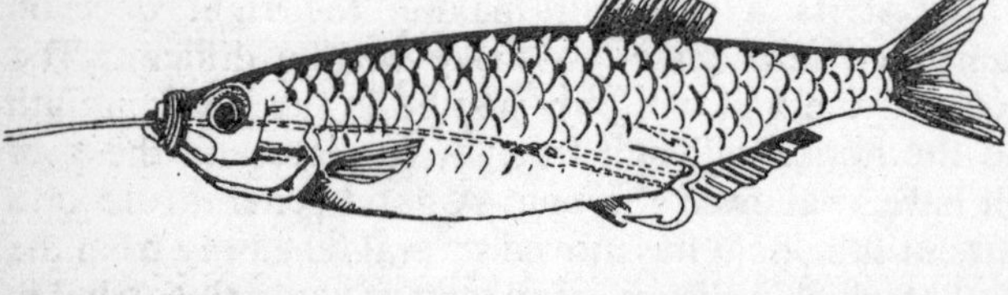

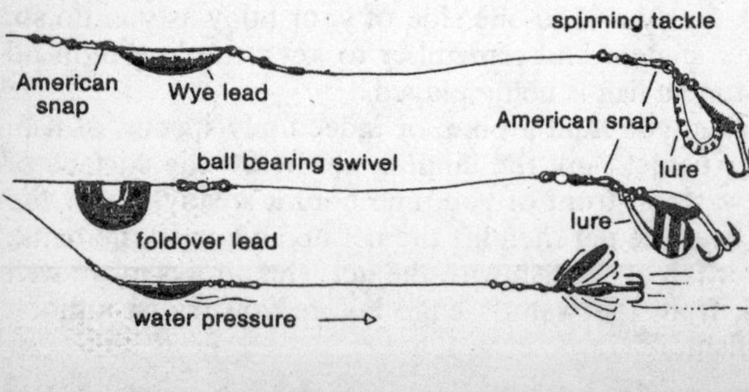

Although most anglers use a dead fish as a pike bait, there is another very sporting form of fishing for them, namely, spinning. Spinners are shaped pieces of metal made in a variety of colours, sizes and designs which flash and twist when drawn through the water. They are attached to the reel line by a metal trace and link swivel, a clip-on device, which helps to prevent the line twisting and so becoming unmanageable. Sometimes lead has to be fastened to the line to help make a long cast, or to get the spinner deep into the water. In my opinion, the most effective spinners are simple spoon shapes in gold and silver colours. They should be worked close to banks, near weed beds and across pools at the tail end of a run.

Cast out, let the spinner sink for a few seconds, then start to wind in. Do this as slowly as possible, but give an occasional spurt, say five or six quick turns on the reel handle. This makes the spinner resemble the swimming action of an injured or sickly fish, something that a pike just cannot resist.

When you have taken one fish, try again in the same area. Often another pike will be found waiting. Remember that these fish are predators – they feed on other fish. To do this they must catch them, and rather than charge around in the water they prefer to lie hidden in weeds – just like carp and tench at times – and dash out from their cover to seize what they recognise as food. Always fish close to their natural cover whenever possible, you may lose some tackle, but the results will be worth it.

Perch, another freshwater predator, can be taken by employing virtually indentical methods, though the tackle should be scaled down as perch are a much smaller species. Often lakes become overpopulated by these sharply aggressive fish, and a lively worm fished on float tackle and cast to areas of a suitable depth such as patches of lily pads, weedbeds, around the staging supports or where reeds fringe margins of waters, can catch fish after fish. However, such fish are not likely to be much larger than 225 g (8 oz). The bigger specimens are more often than not solitary fish which spend their time lurking in sheltered corners.

Sometimes a paternoster rig placed into a gap between the lily beds can be successful, and here the bait can be a worm or even a small sand eel. The latter can be bought frozen from many tackle dealers.

Spinning is an exciting perch-fishing method. A small 'Toby' weedless lure for working around weed beds is excellent, as are lure designs such as Reflex, Ellips and Droppen.

Finally, rudd; a species which some describe as a 'fish for all seasons'. It is often mistakenly described by young anglers as roach, indeed novices of all ages can get the two species mixed. Rudd are very obliging and frequently provide sport during periods when other species seem to have their heads down and be totally uninterested in feeding. The lightest of float tackle, and sometimes an unshotted trace used in conjunction with a self-cocking float, is the way to tempt them. Or a single or double maggot on a 14 or 16 hook, or perhaps a small piece of bread flake or crust, may lure them. Casters can also be deadly, and so can just the tail end of a lob worm.

Rudd bite very smartly, dipping the float in a most positive way, or sometimes no more than a slight sideways movement will indicate that a rudd has stolen the bread paste, or nipped the end off the maggot. Trying to catch rudd on a warm summer day is a delightful pastime, why not try it?

11 Trout Fishing

Richard Barder

Most keen trout anglers spend the winter reading books and magazines about fishing, so that by the time the season opens they are full of theories, ideas and optimism.

However, the cold reality of opening day on a gravel pit or reservoir can be extremely depressing, as the flies about which one has read so much are nowhere in evidence, nor for that matter are the trout. So where do you start?

Pond or reservoir fishing

The first thing to remember is that the fish are probably lying deep. By deep I mean in 1·5 to 6 m (5 to 20 ft) of water rather than 1 m (3 ft). Furthermore, they are likely to be preoccupied with food near the bottom for the simple reason that there isn't much activity near the surface so early in the year.

Common sense dictates the use of a large, interest-provoking lure such as a Jersey Herd. If the water is coloured, which is often the case, then a bright fly is doubly attractive as it is clearly visible. A big fly like a Jersey Herd calls for a stout leader. The fly should be joined by a half-blood knot to 1·2 m (4 ft) of 2·7-kg (6-lb) nylon, which in turn is joined to 1·5 m (5 ft) of 4-kg (9-lb), and the whole is fished on a 'wet' fly line.

It is at this point that the average beginner makes his great mistake. He casts out and as soon as his fly hits the water he starts to retrieve, so the fly comes flashing back several feet above the waving tails of the bottom-feeding trout.

The more experienced man makes his cast, and then allows his line to sink down through the water for several seconds. He starts his retrieve by pulling back line with his left hand in a series of tugs, and at the same time he tensions the line with the thumb and forefinger of his right hand. He will lie his rod tip right down near the water to help keep the line deep, and also take care to keep the rod at right angles to the line and so cushion the nylon leader against the shock of a violent 'take'.

Meanwhile the fly will be inching back just above the bottom in fits and starts, for all the world like some small aquatic creature. Having searched the water to the left of him, the angler will, wind permitting, search the water to his right. Then he will fan his casts out to search the water in front of him. By starting to fish the water close to, there is a chance of taking any fish that may be lurking near by before they are frightened off by movement. During the early part of the season there are often fish to be found right under the bank. Later, of course, the hordes of tramping anglers will have frightened them further out.

My own technique for early season deep-water fishing is to fish deep and recover every cast very slowly, for half an hour or so, followed by fishing deep and a much faster recovery for the next half an hour. If I still hadn't caught a fish I would try a polystickle or Muddler Minnow. If these fail, I would probable try a nymph, which is best fished with a floating line and a 3-m (10-ft) leader. It is important to let the nymph sink right down, and then to retrieve it in very short tweaks, with long pauses between them.

By early May the weather should have warmed up, and the trout be showing on the surface. At this time of year nymphs can bring great success, and it is often possible to plot the course of a cruising fish by his rises, and then drop a nymph just ahead of him. Sometimes it will be taken just as it starts to sink. When using this technique, the nymph is drawn back just under the surface.

On other occasions, when numbers of fish can be seen moving in the same area, it is worthwhile using a floating

The casting sequence for fly fishing

line and slightly greasing the whole of the leader save for the last 60 cm (2 ft). Then, the nymph, which should be a small one, can be inched back in the surface film. The most important point to remember in all nymph fishing is that if your line, leader or fly is causing any wake at all in the surface, you are fishing too fast!

Summer days are not always bright and calm, in fact there will be occasions when there is a fair chop on the water, and few fish will be seen rising. On such a day I would revert to the deep search method, using different speeds of retrieve. Additionally, I would take care to try the water at all depths, as well as right down on the bottom. I have had success on such days by pulling a smallish attractor, such as a Butcher or Dunkeld, through and just below the wave tops.

On a really windy, stormy day, many anglers go home, but I can remember when on one occasion a friend and I took twelve trout, each of 0·45 kg (1 lb) or more, by casting our flies right into the waves breaking against the reservoir dam. We were fishing from a boat, and it was tremendously exciting. One of us had to row his heart out to stop the boat being smashed against the dam, while the other cast his polystickle literally on the edge of the shingle at the foot of the dam. Each time one of us hooked a fish there was even greater excitement, because during the confusion the boat was invariably blown to within metres of the water's edge. I have often wondered what it was the trout were feeding on that day. No matter. If you see big waves breaking and the water stirred up and muddy, cast into the zone where the waves are breaking.

Another occasion when anglers start heading for home is at the end of one of those still evenings when trout are rising everywhere, breaking the calm surface of the water. The fish are probably taking tiny midge pupae in the surface film, and are then extremely difficult to catch. However, just as it gets dark there is usually a lull, followed by the occasional sloshing slurp made by big fish moving. This is the time to oil a big

Sedge, cast it out and tweak it back fairly fast across the surface. The longer the leader, the better, 3·6 m (12 ft) if you can cast it. Failing a Sedge, an Invicta works well, and you should start the retrieve the moment the fly hits the surface.

Yet another occasion which fills most anglers with gloom is the really hot day when not a drop of wind ruffles the surface of the water, which resembles polished pewter. One solution is to go to sleep, but you won't catch any fish! This is the time to fish the deeper water. A nymph fished deep from a floating line, and inched along the edge of a weed bed can be profitable, as can a big lure in more open water. You can tell where the deep water is by using your common sense. Water off the dam, and near pumping stations will be deep, and so usually will an inlet between steep hills. But if the land behind you only slopes gently, then the chances are that it will also slope gently out under the water.

Boat fishing can be interesting if you can manage it, although I'm afraid I belong to that class of angler who seldom remembers to book a boat in time, or lacks the extra money on the day. Nonetheless I have, and do, fish from boats occasionally, and find they can be useful either as a casting platform in a place you like the look of, or alternatively, as a method of fishing the drift. This is a method which probably originated in Scotland where the trout tend to be more surface-oriented, as loch bottoms are often rocky and lacking in rich food. Traditionally, two or three flies are cast in the direction in which you are drifting, so that at any given moment one fly (the tail) is fishing 60 or 90 cm (2 or 3 ft) down, one fly (the dropper) is coming back just below the surface, and the third fly, the bob, i.e. the one nearest the angler, is brought back just dancing through the ripples. The method works equally well in gravel pits and reservoirs south of the Tweed. It is always worth trying to work along one of those calmer wind lanes which can often be seen stretching across the surface of a lake. They show up like a long oily stripe across the surface, and they often contain a bonus of extra fly life. When fishing in any area away from home, you should enquire locally about flies and follow the advice you are given. However, if in complete doubt, you could do a lot worse than put a Black Pennell on the point of your leader, an Invicta on the first dropper and a Butcher or Greenwell on the bob. You can attach the additional two flies by tying the leader in three parts. Each of the two blood knots can be trimmed so that each provides a dropper of 4 cm (2 in). The fly can be tied with half-blood knots to this dropper. The other 'arm' of the blood knots in the leader can be trimmed at about 6 mm (1/4 in) as usual. Fishing three flies or nymphs can lead to tangles. If in doubt use only one fly, as one fished correctly is better than several in a mess.

Boat fishing, reservoir, and gravel-pit fishing have all become highly developed, and in this chapter there is only space to give fundamental instruction. If you want to learn more about lake fishing I cannot give you better advice than to read, mark, learn and inwardly digest everything that is written in T. C. Ivens's *Still Water Fly Fishing* – my own catches improved greatly after a careful study of it!

River fishing

In direct contrast to that which I have discussed so far is river fishing, a sport I consider to be the best of all the ways of hunting for trout.

On big, deep and fast waters you can use a wet fly, dry fly or nymph. On chalk streams, brooks and the smaller tumble-over-the-rocks type of stream, the dry fly reigns supreme as an enjoyable and successful method, but there will also be occasions when a nymph dropped just ahead of a 'nymphing' trout, and then given a little tweak when it is centimetres away from him, will provoke a certain take. This 'induced' take fishing was developed on the Hampshire Avon, and is particularly suited to the crystal-clear waters of our southern chalk streams. It is also particularly suited to people whose casting and eyesight is a great deal better than mine! In passing, and before I forget, I should mention once again that polarised sunglasses which cut out the glare and allow you to see into the water, are an indispensable part of the trout fisher's equipment.

The traditional wet fly river angler casts a team of wet flies, usually three in number, across and slightly downstream. He usually employs a sinking line, and his intention is to work his flies downstream and round, and then gently retrieve them. This method is not suited to clear chalk streams where the fish would undoubtedly see you, and heavy weed growth would make handling the flies difficult, but despite this, in the right circumstances it is a method that will produce fish.

My own view, as I have already suggested, is that there are very few occasions when casting a dry fly or nymph upstream is not the best method.

On chalk streams such as the Kennet, Avon or Test, the technique is to spot the rising fish and then try to drop your dry fly a metre or so upstream from him. The best place from which to mount your attack is from slightly downstream. In this way you will minimise the chances of the fish seeing either you or your floating fly line. The main reasons why many people don't succeed with the dry fly is that they forget that trout have sharp eyes, and that the current may drag their fly round in an unnatural manner. It is no use thundering up the bank until you are opposite a rising fish, and then banging the fly down on his nose, forgetting to throw a little slack in the line to allow for drag, and oblivious to the fact that the fly is skidding across the surface as soon as it hits the water. The trout goes deeper and the angler will think the fish have stopped rising.

There are, of course, many occasions when there genuinely are no fish rising. Nonetheless, they can often be persuaded to rise to a big Sedge thrown beyond them, and then skidded back fast over their noses.

Natural sedges scutter across the surface, and your artificial one can be made to scutter very realistically.

The scuttering Sedge technique is much neglected. It is equally useful at dusk, and triply useful where drag is unavoidable. After all, you are creating drag when you scutter the fly, but to the fishes' eyes the fly is behaving normally. Big trout love Sedges, and I once had trout of 0·9 kg (2 lb), 1·3 kg (3 lb), and 1·8 kg (4 lb) from the same pool by fishing a Sedge with a long leader to minimise the chance of my floating line being seen.

On smaller, rougher streams where the fish are not so visible, it pays to fish your way upstream, just letting your fly drop in all the likely places. Streamy water and anywhere you think the current would carry the natural flies which trout look for are all worth a trial. Remember, if you are wading, move as slowly and quietly as possible.

Hooking, playing and landing trout are largely a matter of common sense and experience. When wet-fly fishing, particularly if you are retrieving your fly fairly fast, there is usually no doubt about the hooking; the fish usually impales itself. There are those who advocate striking again, just to be sure of a well-hooked fish, but I have often seen fish lost because the angler inadvertently lowers his rod, thus giving slack line preparatory to striking again.

Slack line, I believe, is the greatest cause of lost trout, although it is also possible to lose a trout by holding it too hard. If you are using a very small fly you may well pull the hook out, or even open it. If it is attached to fine nylon of around 1·3-kg (3-lb) breaking strain, then there is a good chance that the trout will break the nylon. A sure sign that you are holding a fish hard when on a lake is if it seems to be spending a lot of time on the surface, but a rainbow trout that is lightly hooked will often advertise the fact by jumping a lot. Only you can tell if you are holding it hard, but if you think you are only placing a moderate strain on it, and it jumps a lot, then it is sensible in this case to increase the strain. A lightly hooked fish is one that you want in your net quickly.

Whether you play a fish from the reel or by hand-lining is up to you. Personally, I prefer to recover any slack line the moment I have hooked the fish, and then play it from the reel, but I am well aware that I have occasionally lost a trout while trying to keep up pressure on him at the same time as reeling in slack line. To me, the scream of the reel is more exciting than the hiss of line through damp fingers, but on balance the hand-lining method is probably more efficient.

When river fishing, you should strike as soon as possible, i.e. when the trout can be seen to have taken the fly, or as soon as you feel the pluck of the take when wet-fly fishing. In dry-fly fishing on a fast river you require a very fast strike, but on a slower river you should allow more time. You should also allow more time if you are using a large fly such as a Grey Wulff Mayfly, because trout need more time to get a big fly into their mouths. Incidentally, if you prick and miss a trout there is little point in fishing for it again for at least an hour for although it may continue to rise, it will be inspecting the flies extremely carefully.

When nymph fishing you should strike as soon as you see the trout has taken: this calls for good judgement!

It is worth remembering that a large and lively trout is difficult to bring upstream towards you, and the chances are that it will become entangled in weed. On such an occasion you should try to reposition yourself downstream of the fish. The current will then be helping you rather than the trout and you will have no difficulty in drawing him past the weeds.

The more you can keep out of sight while playing a fish the better chance there is that it won't be panicked into making a last really fast run against a short line. At no time is this more important than at the moment you are landing the fish. In still water the net should be held deep in the water, and the fish drawn over it and lifted clear. River fishing calls for more care. The net should be held downstream of the trout and the fish dropped downstream towards it. Never, never, scoop or dab at a fish; and always try to land the fish yourself. I once nearly lost a salmon through the panicky and misguided efforts of an onlooker.

Although much of your planning and thoughts about fishing will concern actual waterside tactics, it is also worth considering what I call fishing strategy.

I learned a great deal about this aspect of angling when membership of two clubs in the district in which I live gave me the choice of fishing in two rivers, one of which is a chalk stream, the other a fast-flowing brook with boulders, pools and waterfalls, and two lakes. One of the latter was a worked out gravel pit, a few acres in extent; the other an artificial lake fed by a stream.

I soon discovered that the best periods of the day to fish the chalk streams was late morning, and also the second part of the evening when the spent flies were coming down. On the brook, there was always the chance of a fish during the afternoon or evening, though not, curiously enough, during the morning. The brook fish were not concerned with the hatch of any particular fly, but had an eye open for any fly that looked edible.

In the chalk stream the bottom feed and nymphal life were richer, and so the fish could afford to be more selective. On the two lakes, the early morning and late evening were far and away the best periods. Therefore, it will be seen that by careful planning I was able to be in the right place at the right time, and on one fantastic day I ended up with seven large trout. Strategy pays!

Finally, a thought regarding the courtesies of life. Although fishing for trout on lakes and reservoirs can often be obtained on a day ticket basis, you would be surprised how kind the owners of many streams, even favoured chalk streams, can be. The important thing is to ask politely and thank even more politely, both at the time of fishing and also by writing a letter afterwards. The older generation is always impressed by good manners shown by the young, and what's more, such behaviour often brings a further invitation to fish.

12 Sea Fishing

Alan Wrangles

It may surprise you to learn that no matter where you live in Britain, you cannot be more than about 95 km(60 miles) in a straight line from a shore washed by salt water.

The particular area of coast closest to you may not be your idea of the seaside, but for all that, there are probably fish to be caught.

However, there are a number of factors which control the variety of species which you may find in any given place, for despite what some may think, fish are not evenly distributed across the sea bed, and neither are all species found in similar surroundings.

This being so, it is first necessary for the angler to discover that species are where, and at what times they come and go throughout the year. For example: a stretch of coast might, during a 12-month cycle, attract a range of species including mackerel, flounder, bass, cod, plaice, whiting, pouting, eel, mullet, sole, bream and ray. They certainly will not all be present and feeding at the same time, neither will they all take with equal interest the same type of bait. And various methods will be required to catch the fish of your choice.

Consider for a moment a stretch of coastline where, from October to February, whiting and cod are caught, together with reasonable numbers of flounder. The flatfish would, depending on conditions, become scarce as those ready for spawning moved out into deep water from about late January onwards. This would result in very poor angling from February until the March/April period when flounders should start to come back, and they might be joined by plaice at about the same time.

May could see bass feeding along the shore and probably a few eels as well. By June the variety of species could include mullet, plaice, flounder, bass, eels

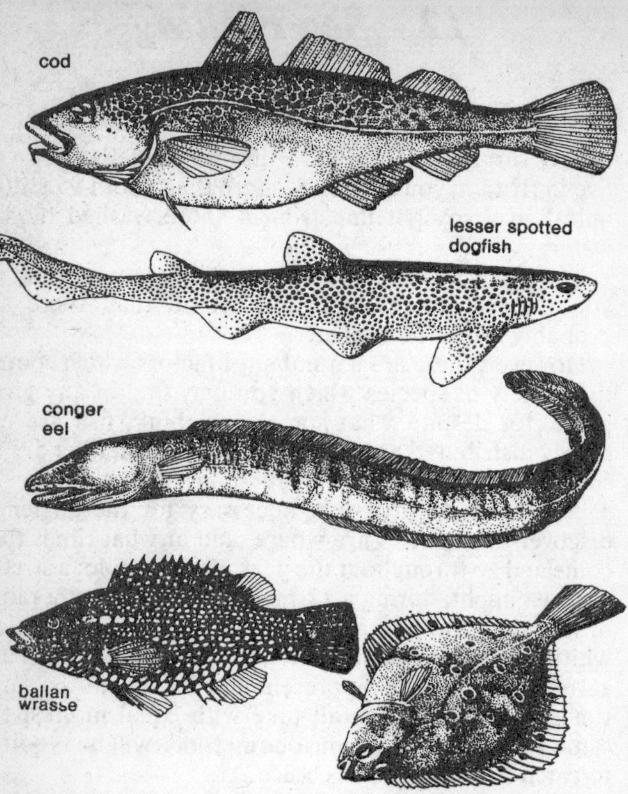

and perhaps even a bream or two. Mackerel could also come close inshore during the summer, and night angling might produce sole and even conger eel.

With the coming of late summer and autumn, bream, mackerel, plaice, sole, mullet and eels would gradually fade from the scene, and by early winter both cod and whiting would come back to rejoin the flounders until they, in turn, went off again for spawning.

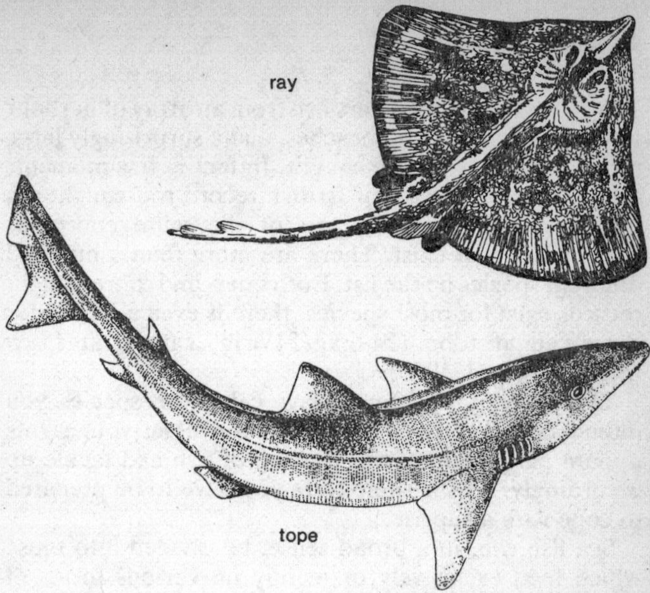

Obviously there are no hard and fast rules relating to either the range of species or the times at which they come and go. Temperature, and also factors such as the type of sea bed, depth of water, and whether or not huge amounts of fresh water from a river are entering the sea can greatly affect both the type and number of fish you might catch.

Flooding, the result of heavy rain miles inland, can send vast amounts of fresh water and debris down into an estuary, and completely upset, for a while, the stocks of sea fish in that immediate area.

Taking other factors such as the natural range of particular species into consideration, it is easy to see that a working knowledge of these factors as they relate to the area you fish is an essential part of being successful. There is no such thing as a consistently lucky angler. The one who continually makes a mark is the angler who studies his craft, and then uses his skills to the best advantage.

Shore fishing

The majority of sea anglers fish from an array of harbour walls, jetties, piers and beaches, and a surprisingly large range of species can be caught. In fact, a few moments spent studying the list of British record rod-caught sea fish will soon convince you of the quite enormous possibilities that exist. There are more than a hundred different species on the list. Both boat- and shore-caught records exist for most species, there is even a record for shore-caught tope (24·6 kg/54¼ lb, caught at Loch Ryan, Scotland, 1975).

Though you will not always catch the species you intend, it makes good tactical sense to set your sights upon a particular species or kind of fish and tackle up accordingly. At the same time you have to be prepared to cope with a suprise.

Sea fish can, in a broad sense, be divided into those which feed exclusively or mainly on various forms of food found on the seabed, and those which will feed at any depth, from the surface downwards.

Two extreme examples are ray and mackerel. Ray such as thornback, blonde, cuckoo and spotted feed almost exclusively on shrimps, sand eels, razor fish, worms, dabs and plaice, species normally associated with life on the seabed. However, mackerel live in shoals and will eat plankton, small fish, shrimps and no doubt many other items which can be taken from the seabed or at any other level at which they happen to be.

Demersal species, that is those which live on the sea bottom, must be fished for in a manner which ties in with their style of living; and hunting pelagic species, or those which frequent various layers above the seabed, calls for a different set of techniques.

Considering the feeding habits of fish can set both the size and type of hook as well as the bait. For example, and taking an extreme case, a size 8/0 forged steel hook baited with a 225-g (8-oz) fillet of fish would not catch a flounder 45 m (50 yd) off-shore. Such a hook and bait

float tackle

wander tackle

spinning rig

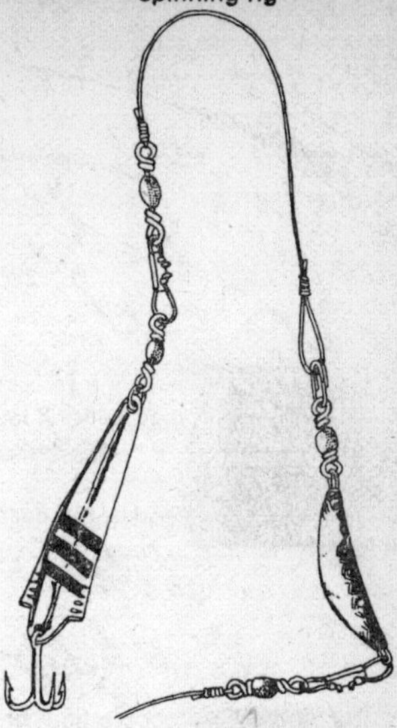

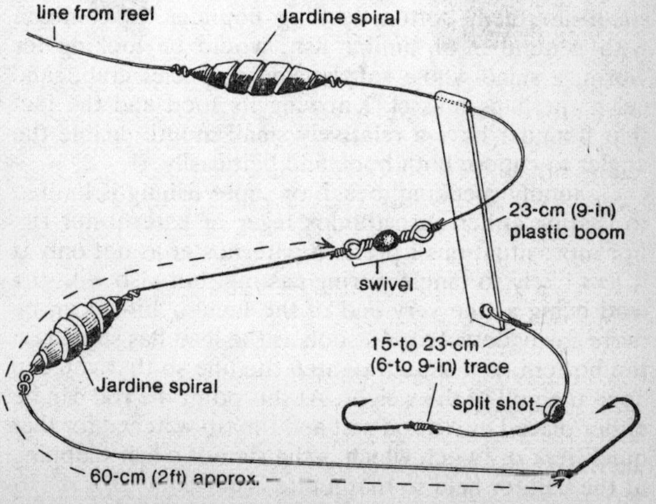

2-hook paternoster using breakaway lead as sinker

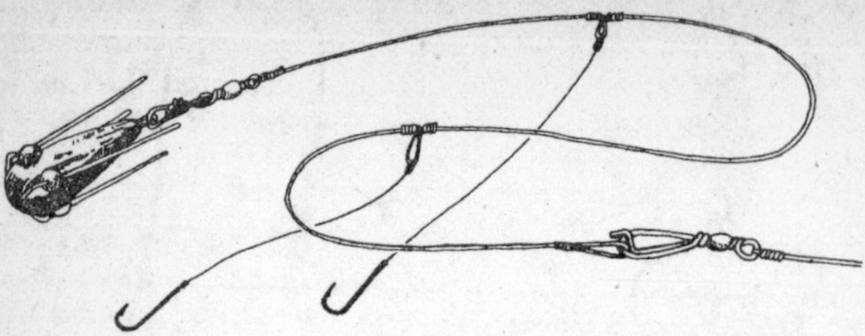

single-hook leger with capta lead as sinker

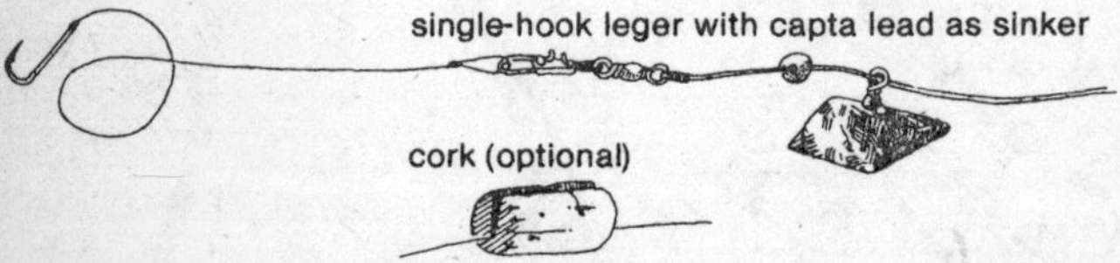

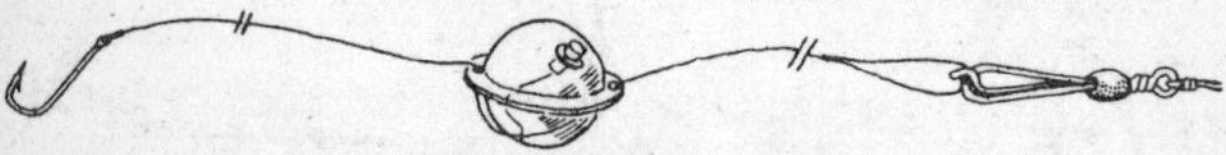

bubble float on leger trace

are more suited to conger, tope or similar species. The small-mouthed, bottom-feeding flounder, in common with a number of similar fish, would be looking for worm, a small whole soft-backed or peeler crab, sand eel or perhaps mussel. Knowing its food and the fact that flounder have a relatively small mouth enable the angler to choose both hook and bait easily.

Generally speaking, beach or shore fishing is limited to casting either an orthodox leger or paternoster rig. For most situations I prefer a paternoster as not only is it less likely to tangle during casting, but also with the lead being at the very end of the tackle, 'bites' can be more easily detected. As soon as the lead has settled on the bottom, you should tighten the line so that you can 'feel' the pull of the weight. At this point the rod can be either placed into a rod rest and the tip watched for that quick jerk or twitch which is the sign of a fish snapping at the bait, or held so that a bite is 'felt'.

Sometimes the rod tip will bend slowly, but very deliberately. This may be no more than the result of a clump of weed fouling the line, but never assume that. It could be the visible sign of a large fish just starting to pull the bait, and if, on holding the rod, you feel definite movement rather than a 'spongy weight' on the line, slip the catch or check on the reel into the 'off' position and let the fish start a definite move which begins to draw line from the spool and then strike.

If the bait is some distance out, say 60 or 70 metres (70 or 80 yards), and there is 110 or 170 g (4 or 6 oz) of lead at the end, the elasticity in the line might well stop you from setting the hook. To counteract this possibility, move up the beach as you strike, which will add force to your action.

I prefer to use a paternoster rig when beach or pier fishing because the fish caught tend to weigh up to 1·3 kg (3 lb). For example, whiting up to 0·9 kg (2 lb), flounders and similar flatfish from 225 g (8 oz) to 0·67 or 0·9 kg (1½ or 2 lb), codling and bass weighing perhaps 1·3 or 1·8 kg (3 or 4 lb), and mullet between 0·4 and 1·3 kg (1 and 3 lb), would be quite a fair average. These fish and those of similar variety and size would send the rod tip into a merry jig, but they are hardly likely to swim away drawing a large lead weight behind them.

However, where it is reasonable to believe that larger fish can be expected, it could be advantageous to use a leger rig. A large fish, for example, a 3- or 3·5-kg (7- or 8-lb) bass, a ray of equal size or larger, or possibly a cod or pollack weighing 5·4 to 6·8 kg (12 to 15 lb) could drag the weight on a paternoster rig into a patch of rock or other hazard where it may snag and be impossible to move. And the fish could well be deterred from taking the bait as a result of feeling the resistance created by the weight of the lead, whereas a fish taking a bait presented on leger tackle should be able to draw line without feeling undue resistance, the lead remaining static until the quarry has been hooked and is being reeled in.

Sometimes it is worth trying a leger with a 'flyer', a system which has advantages when fishing from a pier where really energetic casting is not necessary. However, in such circumstances it is advisable to cast downtide of your fishing position as the current will pull the hook(s) back towards you, creating an impossible angle where the line passes through the eye of the weight boom.

Fishing uptide, as is sometimes necessary, is really better done with a paternoster, but judge either by trial and error or experience, the amount of lead required to hold the tackle in position. If you get this wrong, all the line, hooks, etc., will end up in a tangle around the pier supports, or in some other equally disastrous situation.

You should strike as soon as you judge the fish has taken the bait. Usually there is little or no question of this, for the majority will snap at the food, often impaling themselves in the act. Therefore, a quick response to the dance of the rod tip will set the hook, and barring accidents, the fish is yours. Or is it?

Having hooked it, will you then proceed to lose what you have caught as a result of not making certain that you are in a position to land it?

Never just reel in and hope for the best, particularly when the waves are breaking and sending long fingers of hissing foam racing up the beach. The undertow or back wash as the water retreats can so easily tear the fish from the hook. Or the sudden strain as the line takes the full weight of the fish, lead and maybe some weed, might well result in the line snapping at a weak spot.

So first and foremost, always use a leader of stronger nylon. This will not only absorb the additional strain associated with casting but also take more abrasion as the line is rubbed against rocks and stones by currents swishing along the seabed. A leader should be about twice the strength of the main line, but under exceptional circumstances, for example when an extra heavy weight has to be used, you might find the 'ten times' formula useful. Multiply the weight of the lead by 10, and the result indicates a suitable leader strength.

For most beach fishing situations a 9-kg (20-lb) B.S. main line is adequate, and as a 113-g (4-oz) lead is probably the most widely used weight, an 18-kg (40-lb) B.S. leader is ideal. Around 9 m (30 ft) of leader will usually be sufficient to enable the angler to get the first turn or two on to the spool before the catch is drawn into the surf. The extra line strength prevents many a fish being lost. For landing the fish, a gaff and drop net are vital – a drop net is frequently the only implement that can be used to raise a fish 6 m (20 ft) or so from the sea's surface to the pier deck. For example, mullet, a species with a particularly soft mouth, will usually drop from the hook if they are hoisted, crane-fashion, from the sea.

One of the many advantages of belonging to a club, where pier fishing facilities exist, is that it will have drop nets available for use. You should always drop the net into the water and draw the fish over it.

Landing a fish on a beach when the sea is calm is fairly simple, except if it happens to be a large or dangerous one such as a sting-ray, when a gaff is essential to pull it clear. But you should only gaff a fish you are going to kill, as it damages it.

When a strong wind is sending waves surging up on to the shore, watch how the sea is running. More often than not you will be able to spot a quite obvious pattern. Possibly a series of three or five waves and then a short lull. There could be a pattern in which, every so often, a larger than average wave comes rolling in. Land your fish just in front of the big one and you could be caught by it and swept off your feet. The trick is to play and weaken your fish, and then draw it in, using to full advantage the surge of the biggest wave, and then, if necessary, run back up the beach as you reel in.

Under these circumstances it pays to have a companion with you to gaff the fish, especially if it is a large one. Remember, never place yourself in a position from which it is either impossible or dangerous to land that which you have caught. Every year anglers are swept off rocks and drowned, some while attempting to land a fish.

Always view rocks or any exposed marks with great suspicion. Even during what appears to be the calmest of calm weather, a rogue wave may come surging in to cause havoc and death, particularly along Britain's western coastline.

Spin and float fishing techniques are also used by shore fishermen, but conditions and circumstances need to be right if they are to be really effective. If there is a lot of wave activity, the bait will start jumping about like a dancing puppet; a swift current will either swish the bait towards the surface as the float is held back, or will carry away both float and bait too swiftly. But spin and float fishing can be useful in harbours where species such as bass and mullet feed on the various animals found living in cracks and between stones.

Set the float to present the bait at a suitable depth and allow the current to draw it slowly along the wall. It may be possible to walk with it, and so keep tight control over the tackle, but if you can't, never let a lot of spare line belly out across the surface. If this happen, striking at a bite is delayed, and you will probably miss the fish.

A pier during either the period of high or low water slack might also offer suitable conditions. Keep the bait close to the supports, as fish feed on the various animals that cling to them.

Never use a float which is too buoyant for the bait – remember that a fish will quickly reject a bait that acts strangely. In the case of a float that is over-large for the intended purpose, the bait would be pulled back towards the surface, and the fish would be scared away.

When fishing a mark where either float or spin fishing is possible I always have the necessary tackle assembled and ready for use as soon as the circumstances permit. This is a great time saver, and sometimes enables me to take advantage of an unexpected situation.

This is particularly true of spinning tackle. On one

occasion I was fishing a leger close to the entrance to a small harbour when, without any prior indication, mackerel by the hundred suddenly appeared within yards of where I was standing. My spinner was in the water and amongst the fish in seconds, and although the shoal only stayed fifteen minutes or so, it was long enough for me to catch good-sized mackerel.

On a calm evening, or preferably an early morning, with a tide just starting to make, walking slowly, knee deep along the water line, and casting out and swinging the bait around as you reel in with a start-and-stop irregular action can lure surprisingly large bass.

With all kinds of fishing, never stick rigidly to the strictly orthodox methods. Adapt and innovate, to be able to modify your techniques and so take advantage of every chance. This is the hallmark of a good and competent angler.

Boat fishing

Once afloat, a whole new range of both possibilities and responsibilities applies. First and foremost is safety, without which there can be no successful angling. Although you are probably unlikely to go out fishing in a boat without a grown-up, you ought to know something about it.

A 3-m (10-ft) dinghy is not really suitable for sea angling but a 3·6-m (12-ft) craft will hold two people. Add 60 cm (2 ft) to the length for each additional passenger: e.g. for three, a 4·2-m (14-ft) craft is adequate; for four, a 4·8-m (16-ft) boat is required.

You need British Standard Specification life jackets, a couple of flares or other suitable distress signals, and an alternative means of propulsion – a pair of oars or paddles to get you back if the engine breaks down.

Your boat should have a bailer secured with a length of line so that it cannot be lost overboard. Don't go out in a boat with loose floorboards, don't let your gear roll around, and always see that you have sufficient cable to enable you to anchor anywhere you fish. A free booklet called *Seaway Code* is available from coastguard stations, marine survey offices, public libraries, harbour authorities or direct from the Department of Trade and Industry, Gaywood House, Great Peter Street, London SWIP 3LW, giving much invaluable information regarding taking boats out to sea.

Clothing is another important item. Remember that it is always colder at sea than it is on shore. You will feel a difference only yards away from the beach. As you can always take clothes off if you get too hot tend to over-dress when going afloat, and take a waterproof coat and hat. It is not safe to wear thigh boots in a small boat; waterproof trousers and ankle boots big enough to be kicked off if necessary are the things to wear.

Never set out in a boat without first checking the weather forecast. A tide running westwards, with a breeze in the same direction, will create a nice calm surface. But within a few hours the tide could be running in the opposite direction, and if the strength of the wind increased, you would very rapidly be faced with an awkward, if not dangerous, situation.

Anchoring needs to be done with care and skill. Always have your anchor cable buoyed so that in an emergency it can be slipped and picked up later. Never secure your anchor cable to anything but the correct ring or post in the bow. A cable running out over the side could cause your craft to capsize. When hauling the anchor, do so with the cable coming in over the bow, never the side or stern.

Standing up to play a fish is dangerous, and so is leaning over the side to see what you have caught, or even to net or gaff the catch.

When landing a fish the angler should sit amidships and to one side, with the netsman or gaffer at the stern and on the opposite side. The netsman sinks the landing net and then gives the angler instructions to bring the fish over the net, which is then lifted out and over into

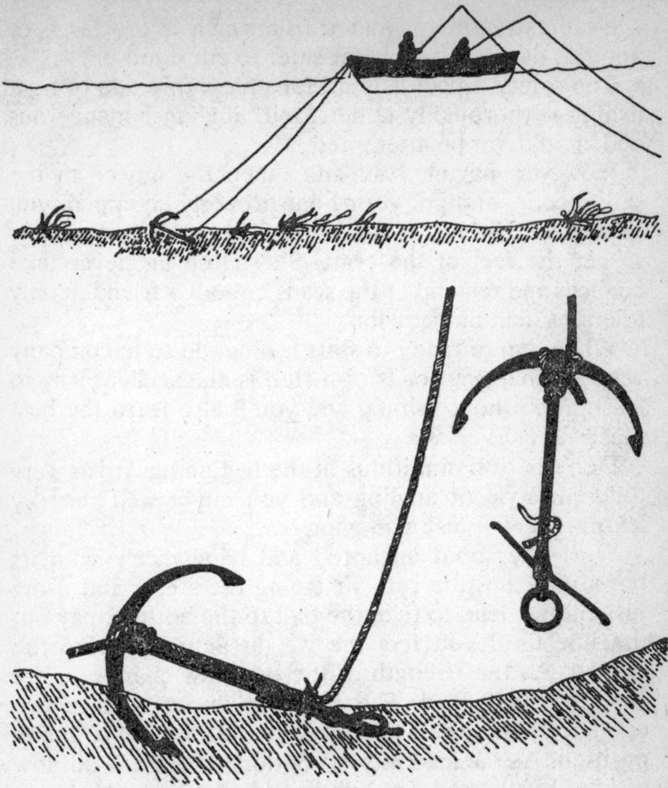

A light line attached to the crown of the anchor allows strain to be put directly on the holding point in the event of snagging the bottom. When fishing a rocky area the anchor rope can be attached to the crown and lashed to the stock with low breaking-strain twine, which breaks with a strong pull and allows the anchor to be drawn out of its hold.

the bottom centre of the boat. You should then release the hook length, move the rod away and deal with the fish correctly, that is, kill it instantly if you are keeping it, or release it.

Never attempt to boat a fish which is too large or appears dangerous. It is far safer to cut it loose.

The safety aspect is vital, for unless this side of boat fishing is thoroughly understood, angling is dangerous and should not be attempted.

However, having read and taken the advice in the safety code, and got your boat properly equipped, you should take it around for a non-fishing trip or two, just to get the feel of the craft. Stay close in, never take chances and remember the sea is nobody's friend, it only tolerates man on occasion.

When you're ready to start fishing, do so in company with another boat or two: a club is an excellent way to learn about boat fishing, and you'll also learn the best places to fish!

Don't be too ambitious in the beginning. It is a very different style of angling and you might well start by learning how to fish a moving bait.

With your boat anchored and lying nicely with its bows into the tide run, sit facing the stern, and using just enough lead to take the bait to the bottom, pay out the line until you feel the weight actually strike the seabed. As the strength of the tide flow changes, alter the amount of lead. The object is always to have just enough to take the bait down, but not to hold it in one position. As the lead hits the bottom, check the outflow of line, lift the rod tip slightly and allow the current to swing the bait and lead up. Hold it stationary for a second or two, and then pay out more line to allow the bait to go to the bottom once again. Keep repeating this movement until the bait is being fished 100 metres or so astern of your craft.

Always maintain a strict control over the amount of line being paid out, as it is essential that the weight of the lead can be 'felt' at all times. If the line is allowed to go slack and belly out in a loop, the pull of a taking fish will be missed.

When using this style, it is often possible to fish with light tackle, even down to a spinning rod, 4·5 kg (10 lb)

B.S. line and no more than a 28-g (1-oz) weight. However, do not forget to change to heavier equipment as soon as conditions warrant it. The terminal tackle can be either an orthodox one-hook leger, or a one-hook paternoster. When fishing light tackle it can be risky to use two hooks as a fish on each could prove impossible to play.

It can be an advantage, especially when fishing for bream, to employ a trace some 1·2 to 1·8 m (4 to 6 ft) long, but fix an anti-kink vane to prevent the trace line twisting.

During both the high and low water slack tide periods, float fishing can be rewarding. Often, during the time when there is very little or no current, fish will come up off the bottom to feed on the various items that may be around. Having first checked the depth, set the 'stop' on the line so that the bait is presented 30 to 60 cm off the sea bed.

Float tackle is also worth trying in places where the tide flow is minimal and crabs are a problem. Adjust the stop to leave the bait a few centimetres above the bottom mud, and let the current do the rest. The technique is similar to that used by a coarse angler fishing a river.

The baited spoon system is an old favourite with inshore anglers, and especially those who fish in estuaries and natural harbours and creeks where wide, snag-free expanses of mud and sand allow the method to be used to its best advantage.

Trail the tackle astern, say 27 m (30 yd) or so, and row slowly with (not against or across) the tide. Make sure the rods and oars have lanyards attached, for a quick snatch by a fish and your rod could be away over the side, and while you are making a grab for the fast disappearing rod, one or both oars could slip out of the rowlocks.

Drift fishing, using wander tackle, is another method which can be used in estuaries or harbours where the bottom is clear. Remember, if the tackle does foul an underwater object, never strain your rod tip by just pulling. Row back over the snag and try to release it with a pull on the line in the reverse direction. If snapping the line is unavoidable, first wrap a few turns around a piece of wood, or a knife handle, and then pull steadily from a sitting position. Never wrap line round your hand or fingers; at best you might suffer a bad cut at worst, amputation!

Sometimes mullet or bass may be discovered feeding around an old jetty or pier, particularly a stone one where cracks and holes give shelter to small animals. It is possible to enjoy a spell of exciting sport by drifting a bait down to them on an un-weighted line.

Anchor up-tide, fix a large float to the end of your line, and let it drift down until it reaches the mark. Tie a stop-knot on to the main line, or fix a short length of elastic band with a slip-knot, at a point midway between the spool and the bottom ring. You now have an accurate gauge of the distance to the jetty. Reel in, remove the float and tie a hook, and if you think it necessary also fix a small bubble float or piece of cork to the line 1 m (3 ft) back from the hook. Bait with a ragworm, sand eel or strip of squid, and let the tide flow carry the tackle along to the fish. Keep the line tight or you will miss the 'take' when it happens. Orthodox leger and paternoster rigs can be used, but remember that large fish such as ray, conger and tope have powerful jaw muscles and teeth which are capable of cutting through single-strand nylon, even if it is 36 kg (80lb) B.S. or more. For large fish, nylon-covered steel traces are essential. However, the species which require such tackle are normally deep-water fish, and are frequently caught by those on board charter boats. These craft, operated by very experienced skippers, are based at many ports around the British Isles.

From Plymouth to Portaferry, and Weymouth to Wick there are opportunities galore to go out and widen your angling knowledge, if you are fortunate enough to be able to do so.

Often it is possible to hire specialist tackle from the

skipper, and this can be checked before you go aboard.

If you are lucky enough to go on one of these boats, it is important to realise that once you leave port you are stuck on board for many hours, so make sure you are well wrapped up and not likely to be seasick.

Fishing in deep water is hard, muscle-stretching work. Frequently 0·45 kg (1 lb) of lead is necessary to get the bait down to the fish. This might mean using either braided or even wire line, ordinary monofilament line would stretch too much and probably not set the hook.

The quite extraordinary power which the tide combined with a fish of 27 or 36 kg (60 or 80 lb) or more can exert has to be felt to be believed. Steel hooks are straightened, and reels not designed to cope with such strains often break or will not work.

Obviously, not all charter boats operate where conditions are so extreme, but you must realise that such possibilities exist, and check before embarking on trips for which you are not equipped.

The less exacting conditions fished by the majority of charter boat anglers call for rods which are matched to perhaps 13- to 18-kg (30- to 40-lb) B.S. line which is loaded on to a multiplier built to hold about 275 m (300 yd). For this type of sea angling tackle needs to be that much bigger and stronger, and where perhaps in shallower waters an American snap was suitable to carry a lead, now a Kilmore or Clements boom is needed.

Despite the stronger tackle, the basic fishing techniques are much the same, except where pirks or similar lures are used. These are kept moving so that the quarry, possibly large pollack, ling or cod, imagines that a small fish is there to be eaten.

There are of course, many other variations on a theme, one never stops learning different ways in which to try to lure the fish one wants to catch.

Sea fishing is not, as I have tried to show, a chuck-it-and-chance-it exercise. It is a sport for the person who wants a challenge, and it is one which, if accepted, can lead to a lifetime of interest and rewarding relaxation.

13 Rules and Regulations

Alan Wrangles

All fishing, both freshwater and salt, is affected in one way or another by laws which, if broken, can bring a variety of penalties.

Bye-laws and regulations relating to freshwater fishing are normally based on the Salmon and Freshwater Fisheries Act, 1975, and sea anglers are, in some ways, governed by the Sea Fishing Industry (Immature Sea Fish) Order (1968), and whatever alterations to this Order are made from time to time.

The principal difference between fresh- and salt-water angling lies in the fact that the former is usually private or is controlled in one way or another, whereas sea fishing is free.

Freshwater fishing

First and foremost, always assume that all freshwater fishing is private, and that you need a permit before starting to fish. Without permission to fish you are a poacher, and that can mean a heavy fine and even confiscation of tackle.

Throughout England and Wales, Regional Water Authorities are responsible for the basic rules by which both coarse and game fishing operate. They enforce 'close seasons' (periods when angling is not permitted), and they also issue rod licences. These allow the holder to fish with a rod and line, but they do not give the holder permission to actually fish in any particular lake or river. Fishing in specific areas is a completely separate issue.

To obtain the necessary permission to go fishing, the angler must either make an arrangement with the person or organisation who owns or controls the fishing rights, or join the group (club or syndicate, etc.) who already have access to the water.

In practice, this generally means either joining a local club or buying a day ticket. The vast majority of coarse anglers belong to organised clubs, as this is by far the easiest way to obtain the sort of fishing you want.

Specialist tackle dealers are, without a shadow of doubt, the best local information centres. Frequently they act as 'recruiting agents' for local clubs, they sell Water Authority rod licences, and frequently have a supply of day tickets or weekly permits for local waters.

All Regional Water Authorities have fishery departments which issue bye-laws. It is your responsibility to know them, ignorance of the law is never an excuse. The bye-laws will set out quite clearly the dates of close seasons, the methods which must not be used, the size of fish which must not be retained in a keepnet, and various other relevant details.

Regional Water Authorities issue angling guides, some of which are free. These publications are all that the average angler needs for initial guidance, as they list clubs, and give excellent information relating to fisheries within the area.

Trout fishing

All the information given under the previous heading regarding rod licences and obtaining permission to fish applies to trout fishing, in fact even more so, as trout waters are very strictly preserved.

Generally speaking, Water Authority reservoirs offer the best chance for relatively cheap trout fishing, in some places it will only cost £2 or £3 per day, sometimes even less for juniors.

For detailed local information consult the Regional Water Authority angling guide. These will always give addresses from which further help can be obtained.

In both Scotland and Ireland there are various rules

and regulations governing the use of rod and line for angling. In Scotland, most fishery rules are designed to protect salmon, but for all that, never assume that either trout or coarse fishing is free. Farmers and landowners do not like people wandering across their land for many reasons, not least of which is the possibility of spreading disease. Never start fishing until you have had permission from the person or organisation controlling the fishing rights.

For trout fishing, as for coarse fishing, local tackle suppliers are a mine of valuable information on all kinds of matters.

Regional Water Authorities

Those of England and Wales are:

North West Water Authority, Dawson House, Great Sankey, Warrington, Lancs. WA5 3LW.
Tel: Penketh (092 572) 4321.

Severn Trent Water Authority, Abelson House, 2297 Coventry Road, Sheldon, Birmingham B26 3PS. Tel: Birmingham (021) 743 4222.

South West Water Authority, 3–5, Barnfield Road, Exeter, Devon EX1 1RE. Tel: Exeter (0392) 50861.

Wessex Water Authority, Techno House, Redcliffe Way, Bristol BS1 6NY. Tel: Bristol (0272) 25491.

Southern Water Authority, Guildbourne House, Worthing, Sussex BN11 1LD. Tel: Worthing (0903) 64571.

Thames Water Authority, New River Head, Rosebery Avenue, London EC1R 4TP. Tel: (01) 278 2300.

Anglian Water Authority, Diploma House, Grammar School Walk, Huntingdon PE18 6NZ. Tel: Huntingdon (0480) 56181.

Yorkshire Water Authority, West Riding House, 67 Albion Street, Leeds LS1 5AA. Tel: Leeds (0532) 448201.

Northumbrian Water Authority, Northumbria House, Regent Centre, Gosforth, Newcastle-upon-Tyne NE3 3PX. Tel: Gosforth (0632) 843151.

Welsh National Water Development Authority, Cambrian Way, Brecon, Powys LD3 7HP. Tel: Brecon (0874) 3181.

Rod licences in Northern Ireland are supplied by the Fisheries Conservancy Board for Northern Ireland, 21 Church Street, Portadown, Co. Armagh.

Although clubs have their own rules which aim to protect both fish and fishermen, sadly there are always a few who break them.

Litter is a problem, it only needs one in a thousand to leave by the water a tin, a plastic bag or a length of nylon complete with hook and shot, and enormous damage can be done.

A sharp-edged tin can cut through a rubber boot, a cow or other valuable farm animal can die as a result of swallowing a plastic bag, and the suffering inflicted on wild birds by carelessly discarded nylon line is horrifying.

An ever-increasing number of clubs rightly follow a very hard line when dealing with anyone who drops litter: instant withdrawal of membership, and frequently no appeal can be made against the decision. Litter is an abomination: never leave any anywhere.

Similar remarks apply to transistor radios in the countryside – many clubs ban them completely.

If you follow the simple rule 'fish as you would be fished by' you will not go far wrong.

Safety is another important factor, as every year there are accidents which need never happen.

When wading, always carry a stick or pole to prod the bottom and so check for ledges, holes or very soft mud. A pole also provides added stability.

Never balance yourself in a precarious position, one from which it would be dangerous, if not impossible, to land your catch.

Always watch out for a stretch of bank which is liable to collapse under your weight. There are few more uncomfortable happenings than being dumped into a metre of cold water on a January morning.

Don't fish alone, and make sure that any younger children with you are never left alone near the water. Always wear non-slip footwear, and if someone does fall into deep water, remember that your landing net, or even a rod, may be sufficient to support or draw them back to the bank.

Finally, and this is most important: never move live fish from one pool or river to another. Frequently this is against the law, as the risk of spreading disease is enormous.

Sea fishing

It is generally accepted that we have the right to fish in tidal waters, except where what is known as a 'several fishery' exists. This means 'distinct', 'separate', or 'individual', and such a fishery is a place where a 'separate' or 'distinct' person or someone given the right by the 'separate' or 'distinct' person are the only ones entitled to fish.

Such places are relatively rare, and are normally well marked and known to local fishermen. Therefore if in any doubt, ask!

Sometimes there are certain restrictions where game fish (salmon and sea trout) and also oysters are concerned, but such places are normally well served by notice boards.

If you are in any doubt, always ask the local Chief Fishery Officer; he can be traced through the telephone directory, local coastguard or harbour master.

However, all these problems can be overcome by either joining a sea angling club (libraries usually list these and other local organisations) or by watching and following local customs and habits.

The majority of sea angling clubs are affiliated to a parent body such as the following:

National Federation of Sea Anglers, 26 Downsview Crescent, Uckfield, East Sussex TN22 1UB

Scottish Federation of Sea Anglers, 8 Frederick Street, Edinburgh EH2 2HB

Welsh Federation of Sea Anglers, 34 Coveny Street, Splott, Cardiff CF2 2NN

Irish Federation of Sea Anglers, 67 Windsor Drive, Monkstown, Co. Dublin

The National Anglers' Council, 5 Cowgate, Peterborough PE1 1LR can also supply information relating to both sea and freshwater fishing.

Frequently shell fish are contaminated, so never collect and eat them. It is best to assume that they should not be collected for human consumption, because even where you see professional fishermen gathering them, it is almost certain that they will be properly cleaned before anyone eats them.

Although not all species of sea fish are protected by the Sea Fishing Industry (Immature Sea Fish) Order (1968), it is generally accepted by those who fish for sport that certain standards should apply to all those kinds of fish that are most usually caught by anglers. Always unhook and return to the sea any fish which are undersize (see overleaf).

Certain fish, for example, weever, stingray and spur dog can inflict wounds which require immediate medical attention as the spines which cause the damage carry venom. Learn to recognise these species and never handle them carelessly. A weever should be pinned down by a boot and the hook cut free after the fish has been killed. Dispose of the body by burying, never just discard it unless you are out at sea.

Stingray have a jagged spike on their tail which they lash over when caught. Pin the body down, kill the fish and cut off the tail before attempting to remove the hook.

Spur dog have a spine by the leading edge of both dorsal fins. Stun and kill the fish, and then remove the spines. These fish are good eating.

Other species, for example, bream, bass and thornback ray have sharp spines on various parts of their

Size limit guide

species	length (nose to tail fork) centimetres	inches
bass	38	15
bream (black)	30	12
bream (red)	30	12
brill	35	14
bull huss	58	23
cod	30	12
conger	71	28
dab	20	8
eel (silver)	30	12
flounder	25	10
garfish	38	15
gurnard	23	9
mullet (grey)	33	13
mullet (red)	33	13
mackerel	28	11
plaice	26	10
pollack	30	12
pouting	26	10
sole	26	10
turbot	40	16
whiting	25	10
wrasse	23	9
skate (common)		2·2 kg (5 lb) weight not
thornback ray		2·2 kg (5 lb) size.

bodies and fins. Always take care when handling sea fish, and never ignore any wound you receive whilst fishing. It is better to be safe than sorry.

And always remember never to fish from exposed rocks or any other position where you can be caught by an unexpectedly large wave. Angling is for fun, not for tragedy.

Disabled anglers

These days there are a considerably large number of angling facilities available for those who are handicapped in various ways. Many clubs and water authorities have created areas which are easy to fish from and simple to approach.

Contact the National Anglers' Council, whose address is on page 131, for full particulars. The Council can also put you in touch with various clubs and associations throughout the country.

Glossary

Anti-kink vane A small 'keel-like' plastic device, fitted with swivels, designed to prevent line twisting and so becoming unmanageable. Half-moon clipover leads can perform a similar task.

Artificial An object made to look like a natural bait form, e.g. a plastic minnow.

Bailiff In the angling sense, a person who guards or in some way protects fish and fishing rights. Some have powers to arrest someone fishing illegally.

Bait box Special container for storing bait.

Bait-box spider A device which screws into the top of a bank stick, and will then hold four bait boxes in a cluster.

Balanced tackle Equipment such as line, reel and rod, with matching or complementary strength – items designed to work together.

Bank stick A metal rod about 1 m (3 ft) long, one end pointed for pushing into the ground, and a female screw thread at the other for accepting a keepnet, bait-box spider, rod rest, etc.

Batting Striking the drum of a centre-pin reel with the palm of a hand and so turning the spool very quickly.

Bead A small plastic ball (various sizes and drilled to accept line) used in the assembly of tackle.

Bob The uppermost of three flies on a three-fly wet-fly cast. The middle fly is called a dropper, the last or bottom fly is the tail.

Canalisation A term used to describe the action which turns a multi-depth meandering stream into a much straightened watercourse with a more even depth.

Casters The chrysalis stage in the development of a fly.

Centre-pin reel A single action reel with a spool set on to a central rod or centre-pin, around which the spool revolves. The most simple of all reels.

Closed-face reel Basically a fixed-spool reel, but the spool is covered, and the line release is trigger operated. These reels are usually fixed in the 'on top' position on a rod, and more often than not, are used when spin-fishing.

Competitive fishing A general term for match fishing. This may mean club v. club, team v. team, or just an individual effort. It is sometimes a mixture of team and individual.

Cooper snap swivel A metal clip with a 'safety-pin' like fastening, and incorporating a swivel, used to assemble, for example, spin fishing tackle.

Crustacea Creatures without backbones and protected by a shell which is replaced as it grows; e.g. lobsters, crabs, shrimps.

Disgorger A metal rod with a shaped end, possibly a 'V' cut, which is used to push against the bend or curve in a hook when set in a fish's mouth. This action presses the hook point out in the reverse direction to which it entered. This device is more commonly used in coarse angling.

Drift fishing Fishing from a boat which is drifting with the tide or wind. Often sea anglers use this style whilst using wander tackle (see page 123).

If it is necessary to slow the drift, a bucket on a line or perhaps a small sack of stones towed through the water will work quite well.

Dropper The middle of a cast of three flies, see **Bob**.

Fixed spool reel A reel with a spool which does not turn whilst delivering or recovering line. The line is laid back on to the spool by a bale arm which revolves around the spool as the handle is turned. This is the most popular type of reel for coarse fishing.

Float cap A small rubber band, usually around the top of the float, used to hold the float in the required position on the line. These can be used around the bottom of the float, then the line need not be passed through the float's 'eye', or bottom ring. By fixing a float in this way, it can be changed without dismantling the whole rig.

Float fishing A style of angling in which a float is used to act as a tell-tale when a fish takes the bait, and to suspend the baited hook at the required depth in the water.

Fly In the angling sense, a fly is a hook or hooks decorated or adorned with various items, e.g., feathers, fur, wool and perhaps silver or gold foil, so that the finished object resembles a natural creature.

Dry flies, those which are designed to float on the surface, are usually formed to imitate an insect which is just hatching, or one which is laying its eggs, dying or which has been blown down or just settled on the water.

Whilst constructing or 'tying' a dry fly, a feather is used in such a way as to make the points or segments stand out, as these points or bristles help the fly to stand up on the water.

Excess water is thrown from the fly whilst casting, but to assist it to float most anglers use a silicone spray, or a similar product, prior to fishing.

Wet flies, or those which are tied to represent a creature which the fish would normally find *in* the water, are, as the name suggests, designed to be fished below the surface. However, there is also another overall, and most important division, among flies, namely 'imitations' (as near as possible) and those which can be described as 'attractors'.

For example, there is the natural mayfly, and the artificial or imitation Mayfly. However, I doubt if anything in nature looks like a 'Fuzzy-buzzy', a fly which is truly an 'attractor'. Indeed, some might argue that the latter is a lure. And in this last category, lures, it is convenient to place items such as wooden plugs which are fashioned to resemble food, for example, a fish. Other lures include artificial prawns, sand eels and minnows.

Fry Young fish newly hatched from the spawn.

Groundbait A substance, e.g. fine bread crumbs, or the minced fish etc, used in a 'rubby-dubby', which attracts fish to a baited hook. Maggots used for this purpose are called 'loose-feed'.

Handlining The recovery of line by hand instead of

using the reel. A method often used by trout anglers, the line being thick and easily managed. A system neither recommended nor practicable for normal coarse or sea angling.

Holdall (rod) A long fabric or plastic container for holding rods whilst travelling. Usually equipped with extra pockets and clips, etc., for holding other items such as landing net and bank stick.

Hooks The only point of contact between angler and fish; they need to be kept clean and sharp. Although a relatively simple item, there are thousands of different designs, sizes and colours. Indeed, one well-known company produces many thousands of different hooks.

For practical purposes, it can be assumed that freshwater hooks start at size 1, and get steadily smaller as they progress to sizes 2, 3 and 4, at which point some types drop the odd numbers and use only even numbers up to size 20, the smallest usually made for everyday fishing.

Sea fishing hooks progress in size from 1 to 1/0, 2/0, 3/0 and so on up to size 20/0.

Basically, you should use the smallest hook which is suitable; and match the size of the hook to the size and type of bait.

Two hooks, fixed back to back, are called a double, three hooks similarly fixed are called trebles.

Jardine snap tackle Two sets of treble hooks, one set fixed, the other adjustable, mounted on fine wire and used for mounting a whole dead fish as bait when pike fishing.

Keepnet A net tunnel several feet long, shaped by plastic rings, used to hold the catch underwater. The top ring has a special fixing complete with thread which screws into the top of a bank stick.

Keepnet stretcher An adjustable metal device designed to extend, and so hold a keepnet fully stretched while it is in use and lying on the bottom.

Leger A style of fishing in which the bait is presented on the bottom.

Line Nylon monofilament is the only line which operates efficiently with a fixed spool reel. This line is made from a single strand as distinct from a multistrand braided line.

Braided terylene line is used by sea anglers, normally whilst fishing in deep water. Monofilament line stretches, and therefore in deep water and where heavy leads are being used, could stretch to such an extent that the act of striking, or setting the hook, would be cushioned by the elasticity in the line.

Braided line is too bulky to be used on a fixed spool reel, and it is both too bulky and rough for use on a multiplier when casting from a beach. Using a thumb to check the fast spinning spool in a multiplier would result in, at best a burn, or more likely a deep cut, if the spool were loaded with braided line.

Fly lines are specially made for specific purposes, and are designed to be matched with particular rods. Briefly, instead of being rated as having a particular strength or breaking strain, e.g., 2·2-kg (5-lb) B.S., a fly line is given a number, e.g., 5, 6, 7 or 8. Fly rods are graded in a similar way, e.g., 5 or 6 class, which would match a number 6 line. A light trout rod would be classed as a 5, a heavy salmon fishing rod a 12, and so matching lines are essential for efficient casting.

Fly lines are also graded according to whether or not they float or sink (dry or wet lines) and also according to their shape. For example, a line which tapers at both ends is called a double tapered line, and is given a DT marking. Another style of line, which has all the weight at one end, is called a weight forward or WF line. A line marked DT 6 F would be a floating or 'dry' line, double tapered and 6 weight. A 'wet' line is identified by the letter 'S' (sinking).

Many other fly lines are made, for example, fast sinking, slow sinking, floating but with sinking tip, etc. General fishing experience will teach you which to use and where.

Litter Never discard hooks, old lengths of nylon, plastic bags or any other item which will cause death and/or suffering to wild animals, or merely disfigure the seashore or countryside. Litter is an abomination, avoid it at all costs. Dropping litter can also cost you your fishing privileges.

Lure See under **Fly**.

Mark A term used to denote a particular place to fish; normally associated with sea fishing.

Match fishing See **Competitive fishing**.

Mollusc Invertebrate animal (i.e. one without a backbone) having a soft fleshy body and usually a hard shell, such as mussels and snails.

Mucilin A trade name for a floatant which can be applied to a line or fly.

Nymph An immature form of insect which resembles the adult yet lives differently. For example, the mayfly nymph lives in the mud at the bottom of a river. Anglers use imitation nymphs when trout fishing.

Paternoster A special method or style of angling in which the line runs directly from rod tip to a weight at the end. The hook(s) and bait(s) are fixed to the line above the weight. A short length of line carrying the hook(s) would be called a *trace*, or *snood*, the latter being a sea angling term.

Point The last two or three feet (approximately) of a tapered fly cast.

During the course of fishing and changing flies, the point is gradually shortened; and therefore, every so often, a new point must be tied. For this a blood knot can be used (see page 75).

Priest A short stick, weighted at one end, used for killing fish.

Quiver tip Short length of stout but flexible nylon with a top ring at one end and screw adaptor at the other. The tip screws into a special top ring on a rod, and the main line then runs through the tip ring. Used when leger fishing, the quiver tip acts as a bite indicator.

Rising Fish are said to be rising when they can be seen taking items of food from the surface.

Rods Modern rods normally fall into one of two categories: solid or hollow (tubular).

Most anglers still use what are called solid glass or hollow glass rods, although carbon fibre is slowly becoming more widely used. (The cost of carbon fibre is a deterrent to some).

A 'solid' glass rod is basically a tapered rod made of resin in which are embedded glass fibres. The taper or general shape of the rod determines its strength, casting ability and 'action', in other words how it bends or acts whilst under stress.

A 'hollow' glass rod is made by wrapping resin-coated glass cloth around a shaped steel rod (a mandrel), which is then baked or 'cured' in an oven.

The rod designer, by setting specific lengths, thickness of cloth, etc., then produces a rod for a particular style of fishing.

Generally speaking, the final price you pay for a rod is decided by the quality of the materials used to make it, and by the standard of the fittings, such as the rod rings.

Rod rings The fittings on a rod which both direct the line from reel to rod tip, and also transfer the strain on the line to the rod.

Rolling leger Leger tackle using a ball- or bomb-shaped lead which, under the influence of current or tide, will roll along the bottom.

Rules Always assume that all angling is governed by rules of one kind or another.

In sea angling, although access to and casting from a beach may be free, there are size limit rules which prohibit the taking of certain species, e.g., cod, whiting, plaice, if these fish are below a certain size (see pages 131–2). Fish smaller than the permitted size must always be returned to the sea.

Local tackle shops and clubs will give advice regarding size limits, and often at recognised angling centres such as piers and harbours, or places where professional fishing boats operate, official Ministry of Agriculture

Fisheries and Food posters are displayed showing the 'official' size limits.

Coarse fishing is governed by the various rules set down by the relevant water authorities, and also the clubs and/or owners of the fisheries.

The rules include times during which you may or may not fish, prohibited methods or styles of fishing, and also size limits. These can vary from area to area. For example, in the South West Water Authority (Cornwall Division), there is no statutory close season for coarse fishing, a situation which recently has been extended to include the Devon Division.

Always make sure that you know the local rules and regulations before starting to fish.

Trout fishing is also subject to a variety of rules. Most fisheries have what is known as a 'limit bag', perhaps a maximum of four or six fish. In other words, you are not permitted to catch and keep more than the bag limit of sizeable fish, and once you have taken this number you must stop fishing. At some fisheries you must kill all trout you land.

Most trout fishery rules prohibit the use of 'bait', that is, worm or maggot, etc., and spin fishing is often banned. However, this isn't always the case.

Close seasons vary, for example in the Southern Water Authority area all trout fishing ends on the last day of October, but in the South Western Water Authority region it is possible to fish for rainbow trout up to Christmas at some reservoirs.

The angler is responsible for knowing and keeping to the rules, so always make sure you know the rules before you start to fish.

Shock The sudden strain on a line or rod created by casting or striking at a taking fish.

Side strain Some fish, when hooked, will head straight for a weed bed or other hazard. It is often impossible to stop a large fish, e.g. a 9-kg (20-lb) carp, from getting into a clump of water plants unless it is turned away from its intended course. But by laying the rod tip over to left or right the angle of strain is changed from above to the side.

Side strain will often turn a fish, whereas a direct overhead stopping action could result in failure of line or hook hold.

Spinning A style or method of angling used to catch predatory species such as pike, perch, mackerel, bass, etc., in which a device made to attract fish is fitted with hook(s), and is drawn at varying speeds through the water.

Spinners and other similar devices such as spoons, plugs and pirks are given a variety of names such as Toby, Ellis, Atom, Vibrax and Rapalo.

Split ring A small version of a well-known item – frequently used as a key ring – employed by anglers to assemble tackle. A split ring might be used to join a treble hook to a spinner or plug.

Split shot These are pellets of soft lead, deep and sharp cut so that they can be pressed around fishing line. They provide the weight necessary to take a baited hook down to the required depth. The smallest, dust shot, is the start of a number of sizes, ranging from 6, 5, 4, 3, 2, 1, BB, AA, AAA and on to the largest, SSG.

Spring tip A device similar to a quiver tip.

Stop A device, possibly a knot or split shot, placed on a line to prevent another item, such as a float, from passing a given point.

Strike The response to a bite is a 'striking' action, or lifting the rod tip to tighten the line and so drive the hook into the fish's jaw.

Swim The particular area being fished by one angler.

Swing tip A bite indicator used when leger fishing. A short flexible length of stout nylon, similar to a quiver tip but joined to the rod tip by a flexible joint so that it swings or lifts as a fish bites.

Swivel A small item of tackle with a ring at each end which can turn or swivel, each independent of the other. Swivels are used to assemble tackle, particularly spinning rigs, or where movement may impart 'twist' to the line.

Test curve The strain (described in a measurement of weight) needed to pull a rod tip over to an angle of 60°.
Trace length A short length of line carrying the hook. See **Paternoster**.
Trotting down A float fishing technique used in moving water. The float carries the baited hook downstream for a distance set by the angler. It is sometimes called 'trotting' or 'trotting the stream', also 'long-trotting' or 'long-corking' if the distance being covered is that much greater.
Wander tackle This is a particular style of arranging tackle, and it is an excellent method for taking flounders. Developed by the late Mr Percy Wadham, it consists of a plastic or metal boom (about 22 cm/9 in long) attached to the end of the reel line. At the free end of the boom is fixed a 15- to 22-cm (6- to 9-in) trace and hook, and another trace – about 60 cm (2 ft) long – is tied to the boom where it is fixed to the main line.

A Jardine spiral is fastened on the main line immediately above the boom, and another about half-way down the longer of the two traces. Both hooks are baited, and fishing takes place while drifting, or the angler casts and recovers very slowly, pausing after each turn or two on the reel handle.
Zander A freshwater species imported from Europe during the 1870s, and released into the lakes at Woburn Abbey. Since then, this predatory species has spread to some limited extent, but the continued expansion of their range is generally resisted as they can displace our native species. Zander can grow to around 18 kg (40 lb), in weight but at the time of writing the British rod caught record was 7·7 kg (17 lb 4 oz).

More Beaver Books

We hope you have enjoyed this Beaver Book. Here are some of the other titles:

The Beaver Book of Lists A Beaver original. The highest mountains in the world, the most hated school dinners, favourite football players – a collection of useful and useless information on all kinds of subjects that makes absolutely compulsive reading. Compiled by Hunter Davies and illustrated with amusing cartoons by Graham Thompson

The Beaver Book of Bikes A Beaver original. Packed with information on everything you need to know about bicycles – from buying, maintenance and restoration to games, activities and the history of bikes – this book is written by Harry Hossent and illustrated with drawings by Peter Gregory and cartoons by Maggie Ling

Ed at Large When Ed hunts for news for the *Baker Street Bugle*, his school magazine, he gets into one scrape after another. The hilarious adventures of this modern-day 'William' are described by Tom Tully, author of *Little Ed*, and illustrated by Lesley Smith

These and many other Beavers are available from your local bookshop or newsagent, or can be ordered direct from: Hamlyn Paperback Cash Sales, PO Box 11, Falmouth, Cornwall TR10 9EN. Send a cheque or postal order, made payable to the Hamlyn Publishing Group, for the price of the book plus postage at the following rates:
UK: 40p for the first book, 18p for the second book, and 13p for each additional book ordered to a maximum charge of £1.49;
BFPO and Eire: 40p for the first book, 18p for the second book, plus 13p per copy for the next 7 books and thereafter 7p per book;
OVERSEAS: 60p for the first book and 18p for each extra book.

New Beavers are published every month and if you would like the *Beaver Bulletin*, a newsletter which tells you about new books and gives a complete list of titles and prices, send a large stamped addressed envelope to:

Beaver Bulletin
Hamlyn Paperbacks
Banda House
Cambridge Grove
London W6 0LE

202070